THE COMPLETE IDIOT'S GUIDE® TO

Tapas

by Jeanette Hurt

ALPHA

A member of Penguin Group (USA) Inc.

This book is dedicated to my parents, Tom and Mary Hurt, and my sisters, Julie and Karen Hurt. I will never forget traveling through Spain with you.

ALPHA BOOKS

Published by the Penguin Group

Penguin Group (USA) Inc., 375 Hudson Street, New York, New York 10014, USA

Penguin Group (Canada), 90 Eglinton Avenue East, Suite 700, Toronto, Ontario M4P 2Y3, Canada (a division of Pearson Penguin Canada Inc.)

Penguin Books Ltd., 80 Strand, London WC2R 0RL, England

Penguin Ireland, 25 St. Stephen's Green, Dublin 2, Ireland (a division of Penguin Books Ltd.)

Penguin Group (Australia), 250 Camberwell Road, Camberwell, Victoria 3124, Australia (a division of Pearson Australia Group Pty. Ltd.)

Penguin Books India Pvt. Ltd., 11 Community Centre, Panchsheel Park, New Delhi—110 017, India

Penguin Group (NZ), 67 Apollo Drive, Rosedale, North Shore, Auckland 1311, New Zealand (a division of Pearson New Zealand Ltd.)

Penguin Books (South Africa) (Pty.) Ltd., 24 Sturdee Avenue, Rosebank, Johannesburg 2196, South Africa

Penguin Books Ltd., Registered Offices: 80 Strand, London WC2R 0RL, England

Copyright © 2008 by Jeanette Hurt

International Standard Book Number: 978-1-59257-824-5
Library of Congress Catalog Card Number: 2008927336

10 09 08   8   7   6   5   4   3   2   1

Interpretation of the printing code: The rightmost number of the first series of numbers is the year of the book's printing; the rightmost number of the second series of numbers is the number of the book's printing. For example, a printing code of 08-1 shows that the first printing occurred in 2008.

Printed in the United States of America

Note: This publication contains the opinions and ideas of its author. It is intended to provide helpful and informative material on the subject matter covered. It is sold with the understanding that the author and publisher are not engaged in rendering professional services in the book. If the reader requires personal assistance or advice, a competent professional should be consulted.

The author and publisher specifically disclaim any responsibility for any liability, loss, or risk, personal or otherwise, which is incurred as a consequence, directly or indirectly, of the use and application of any of the contents of this book.

Most Alpha books are available at special quantity discounts for bulk purchases for sales promotions, premiums, fund-raising, or educational use. Special books, or book excerpts, can also be created to fit specific needs.

For details, write: Special Markets, Alpha Books, 375 Hudson Street, New York, NY 10014.

Publisher: *Marie Butler-Knight*
Editorial Director: *Mike Sanders*
Senior Managing Editor: *Billy Fields*
Acquisitions Editor: *Michele Wells*
Development Editor: *Ginny Bess Munroe*
Production Editor: *Megan Douglass*
Copy Editor: *Nancy Wagner*

Cartoonist: *Chris Sabatino*
Cover Designer: *Bill Thomas*
Book Designer: *Trina Wurst*
Indexer: *Angie Bess*
Layout: *Ayanna Lacey*
Proofreader: *Laura Caddell*

Contents at a Glance

Contents

Appendixes

Foreword

Tapas, tapas ... they're everywhere nowadays. You can't go out without seeing "small plates" on the menu, whether you're at that hip new restaurant in town or the local chain down the street.

We all know that tapas are a great way to sample the food at your local eatery, but there is a lot of mystery as to where these little snacks started. Some say that in the arid climate that surrounds Andalusia, in southern Spain, it was a way for bar owners to cover the drinks of patrons and keep out bugs and dust. Tapas also had the benefit of stimulating the appetite for drinks, as most of the staples (such as ham and/or cheese on bread) were salty. As time passed and competition grew, tapas became more elaborate to draw guests in the door. Others say that tapas were created by an edict sent down by the king when he had fallen ill. It was said that to remedy his health, the king would drink wine with small bites many times a day. After he had recovered, he made it a law that no wine should be served without something to eat with it.

No matter how they began, tapas are a fun and adventurous way to sample the many different flavors of Spain. Most Spanish bars, restaurants, and ma-and-pa shops have a selection. Some places put out an elaborate spread where people pick and choose what they want as it sits on ice behind glass. Some places specialize in only one thing, which they do very well. Others let you choose from a board what you want the kitchen to send out. Yet they all have one thing in common: the act of sharing these small plates helps to stimulate conversation and bring together the people huddled around them. Known as *tapeo* (basically a glorified pub crawl), a group of people meet at a tapas bar just long enough to grab a quick snack and glass of wine or sherry. Then, before the stools below them have even warmed, they move on to the next bar to sample new wares.

This book is a great way to start your *tapeo*, or journey into this world of small plates. By no means is this book meant to be a be-all, end-all of tapas, as no book ever could be. Instead, it is meant to be a foot in the door—a way to sample the huge variety of flavors from all over Spain, from the olive oil and garlic used in the hot south to the inventive combination of meat and seafood in Catalonia, to the more temperate north where apples, cabbage, and beef are abundant. It is a way for you to see the interesting flavor combinations, fantastic ingredients, and proof that Spain stands up to other gastronomic giants like France and Italy when it comes to the contribution it has made to the culinary world.

Tyge Nelson
Executive Chef
Solera Restaurant
Minneapolis, MN

Introduction

Tapas are the savory and sweet appetizers of Spain. But to call them just appetizers belies their importance. For in Spain, tapas aren't just hors d'oeuvres, they are a way of life. Culturally significant and culinarily delicious, tapas are small dishes, meant to be shared among friends and family members. They are not just about eating—they are about experiencing the food with loved ones.

Tapas—and small plates in general—are more popular than ever before, and the necessary Spanish ingredients are more easily available than ever before. This book will share with you the history of tapas, and it will also show you how to make the most popular tapas dishes. It will also explore the culinary regions and important Spanish ingredients, as well as teach you some professional cooking techniques that will make your time in the kitchen more enjoyable.

The Complete Idiot's Guide to Tapas will help you make these delectable dishes like a pro, and because you're making them yourself, they will probably taste even better because you made them. There are plenty of recipes in here—more than 100, in fact—for hot and cold dishes, as well as the sweet and savory ones. It is a book to use, and if you enjoy it, by the time you finish it, it might even have a few smudge marks and corners turned down—the sign of a well-used cookbook.

And because tapas is never served without sangria or wine, and every tapas meal should be capped off with a delicious treat, this book will also introduce you to Spanish wines and desserts, too. Happy eating!

How to Use This Book

It may be trite, but the best place to start is at the beginning. **Part 1, "Introducing Tapas,"** covers just that. It not only introduces you to the history of tapas and Spanish cuisine but also introduces you to the key Spanish ingredients and cooking techniques that will make preparing tapas a breeze. Everything in this section better helps you prepare the recipes in later chapters.

Part 2, "Cold Tapas," teaches you how to make the delicious appetizers that are best served chilled. This section also introduces you to some quick and easy, virtually no-cook tapas.

Part 3, "Hot Tapas," tackles the techniques and recipes for creating delicious tapas that are best served warm and fresh out of the frying pan.

Part 4, "The Good Life: Sweets, Drinks, and Party Tips," shows you how to throw a great tapas party, but it also introduces you to Spanish wines and sangria, as well as caps off your eating experience with some decadent desserts.

Extras

I have to admit—I'm a tapas geek, and I dearly love to share my knowledge and spread my enthusiasm to anyone who cares to listen. For your special benefit, I've added some interesting tidbits and facts in each chapter, which you'll find under these headings:

Hablo Tapas

Words that might be unfamiliar to you but are frequently used in Spanish are defined here.

Hot 'n' Spicy

These are warnings about challenging or confusing details in making tapas, with tips on how to identify snafus and how to avoid them.

Tapas Tricks

The hints and tips in these boxes make cooking easier and also sometimes offer some ideas for varying a recipe.

Appetizing Extras

This is a space for little bits of interesting information. Enjoy the trivia on its own—or impress your friends with your new-found knowledge.

Acknowledgments

I could not have written this book without the loving support of my husband, Kyle Edwards. Nor would it have been as good without the generous sharing of recipes from several chefs, including: Emilio Gervilla of Emilio's Restaurant in Hillside, IL; Matthew Silverman, of Vintner's Grill in Las Vegas; Gregg DeRosier of the Anaba Tea Room in Milwaukee; and Dan Smith of McCormick & Schmick's Seafood Restaurant in Milwaukee. The Foods from Spain and the Trade Commission of Spain, especially Mercedes Lamamié, as well as Kristina Peterson, of Weber Shandwick, and Marisa Baile, also of Weber Shandwick provided much help and useful information. I am extremely thankful to Ana Porres and the Tourism Office of Spain in Chicago, along with all of my hosts in Madrid, Segovia, and Toledo, especially Cristina de Hevia. Many of the beautiful photos in this book were taken by John Braun, a talented photographer who also happens to be married to Dena Braun, an equally talented writer (Check out more beautiful photos of Spain at www.fitglobetrotter.com). I also owe a huge debt of gratitude and a pitcher of sangria to the "Kitchen Chicas," my dear friends and family members who either graciously allowed me to include their recipes or who helped me test my recipes: Sarah Dowhower, Marcie Hutton, Karen Hurt, Tamara Johnston, Karen Malhiot, Julie Neubauer, Ranjana Patnaik, Jeanne Potter, Lisa Stardy, and Amy Vuyk. Thanks to Damon Brown, my writing buddy, Marilyn Allen, my fantastic agent, and my wonderful editor, Michele Wells and the other talented people at Alpha Books including development editor Ginny Munroe, production editor Megan Douglass, and copy editor Nancy Wagner. I would also like to thank Ramona Serrandilla, who taught me what real *tortilla Español* should taste like.

Special Thanks to Technical Editor

Tyge Nelson reviewed *The Complete Idiot's Guide to Tapas* and double-checked the accuracy of what you'll learn here, to ensure that this book gives you everything you need to know about tapas.

Trademarks

All terms mentioned in this book that are known to be or are suspected of being trademarks or service marks have been appropriately capitalized. Alpha Books and Penguin Group (USA) Inc. cannot attest to the accuracy of this information. Use of a term in this book should not be regarded as affecting the validity of any trademark or service mark.

Part  1

Introducing Tapas

In Part 1, we take a look at the history of tapas and the culinary traditions of Spain. Knowing a little bit about Spain's culinary roots will help you better enjoy tapas. We also cover the basic ingredients you'll need to stock your Spanish pantry and give some tips and basic culinary techniques to make preparing tapas more enjoyable. If you are already a pro in the kitchen and quite familiar with Spanish culture, you may not need all the information in this part, but do skim through it anyway. You might learn something new.

Chapter 1

Of Tapas and Traditions

In This Chapter

◆ Cultural and historical influences on Spanish cuisine

◆ History of tapas

◆ Culinary regions of Spain

Nothing is quite like tapas. These savory little dishes from Spain are becoming more and more popular, and as food trends for the new millennium go, expect this trend of "small plates" to definitely continue.

Ever since I lived in Spain, I've been enamored with these delicious, little delicacies. But because I have not always lived in close proximity to a good Spanish restaurant, I have had to learn the intricacies of making these wonderful appetizers to satisfy my odd craving of *ensalada rusa* (Russian potato salad) or *empanadas* (stuffed pastries).

As Spanish food and tapas have grown in popularity, so has the availability of quality Spanish ingredients. I no longer have to search for real Spanish paprika. Because it is now relatively easy to get the proper ingredients, with a little know-how, it's also easy to get your tapas game on.

This chapter introduces you to Spain's diverse culinary heritage—a mélange of European, Roman, Moorish, and New World influences. It also explores Spain's culinary regions.

Spain's History and Culinary Influences

Way back in Spain's history, before Rome was even Roman, Spain had been variously conquered, settled, etc., by the Phoenicians, the Carthaginians, and the Greeks, all of whom had spent some extensive time in Spain.

Then, those conquering Romans came along, built their roads and aqueducts (one immense version you can still see in Segovia), and also brought along their foods. Most specifically, these Roman soldiers brought the olive tree and planted them across the Iberian Peninsula. Today, if you travel in Spain, you'll find olives galore throughout the countryside, and almost all Spain's dishes involve olive oil. (This generally applies to the south and central parts of Spain, not as much in the north. Butter is generally used as it is a much more temperate climate.) The Romans also introduced wheat to Spain and brought along their wine and winemaking techniques, although wine dates back to an even earlier time in Spain.

Then the Moors moved in and spent more than 700 years in Spain. Even though the Europeans finally managed a reconquest of the country, the Moors left an indelible influence on Spanish culture, particularly, its cuisine. They introduced Spain to spices—saffron, cumin, and cinnamon, along with anise, nutmeg, and black pepper. They also brought the many citrus fruits used in Spanish cooking to this day and introduced sesame seeds and rice as well.

Now, things get even more complicated when you realize that the Celts settled in northwest Spain in Galicia, the Basque people settled along the Pyrenees in Pais Vasco (Basque Country in northern Spain), and the Catalans settled along northeast Spain in Catalonia.

Then just for more fun, add to the mix the Spanish conquistadors, who explored the New World, North and South America, and brought back intriguing plants and foods, such as chocolate, tomatoes, potatoes, and peppers.

What this means is that culturally speaking, Spain has had a
variety of influences, making it
the unique place it is today.

What adds to its uniqueness
is its geography. The Iberian
Peninsula connects the Atlantic
Ocean with the Mediterranean
Sea in southwestern Europe,
making it a very coastal region.
As such, seafood plays a big role
in Spanish cuisine.

> **Appetizing Extras**
>
> Celebrated Spanish
> cookbook author Penelope
> Casas explains Spanish culi-
> nary influences in this way:
> "Trendy 'fusion cooking' that
> today excites our taste buds
> has, in fact, been the essence
> of Spanish cooking for almost
> 2,000 years."

Finally, Spain is the third largest country in Europe in terms of landmass. It has many mountains, and while the climate is a bit drier than
the rest of Europe, it has great soil, which has led to great, and diverse,
agriculture.

Now, what does this have to do with cuisine or more specifically, tapas?
Everything. The imprints of these various peoples and geographic con-
siderations can be tasted in the tapas dishes. As different ethnic groups
conquered and settled Spain, their various traditions were filtered and
passed down through generations.

Tapping into Tapas History

Tapas, as a cultural dish, goes back to at least the nineteenth century,
and various legends and stories explain how it became the culinary
phenomenon that it is today.

Several tapas stories revolve around Castille's King Alfonso X, also
known as Alfonso the Wise. Apparently, this Castillian monarch took
ill at some point during his thirteenth century reign, but he was able to
recover by eating smaller portions and consuming them with that modern day elixir, wine. His subjects then adopted his eating habits. Other
stories suggest he decreed that taverns should serve small portions of
food with liquor.

Another legend involving Alfonso sets the tapas tale in Andalusia.
While traveling, he stopped at an inn in Cadiz where he was served a

glass of sherry. The winds had kicked up a storm that day, so the savvy innkeeper protected the king's drink by topping it with a piece of ham. When the king ordered a second glass, he requested another cover or *tapa* with it.

Hablo Tapas

Tapar is the Spanish verb for to cover, and *tapa* is the noun for cover or lid. *Tapas,* therefore, is the plural form of the noun.

A more likely yet less romantic origin, however, is that the tapas tradition began with Spanish bartenders who served their patrons wine or beer with little lids, pieces of bread topped with tiny bits of ham, sausage, or cheese.

The bartenders employed these edible coverings to protect the wine from pesky fruit flies, and the food also helped to prevent their clientele from becoming too inebriated. Conversely, because the complimentary appetizers were salty, their patrons were thus encouraged to drink more in order to quench their thirst.

According to noted Spanish cookbook author Penelope Casas, the tradition of tapas most likely originated in Andalusia in the nineteenth century and was entwined with sherry consumption. Because sherry has a higher alcohol content than wine, it usually is sipped as an aperitif rather than as a dinner accompaniment. "As such, it cries out for a tapa of some kind," Casas says.

The other reason Casas believes tapas began in the South of Spain is that its inhabitants embody such a spirited approach to life in general. "Nowhere in Spain is there more joie de vivre than in southern Spain," Casas says. "Tapas and the conviviality they embrace are an essential part of (an Andalusian resident's) social world."

The Spanish Style of Eating

Tapas are an integral part of a Spaniard's way of eating. In fact, without them, many Spanish folks might get too hungry between lunch and dinner.

In Spain, eating well is almost as important as breathing. Not to eat well is unthinkable. Eating is an all-day-long sort of affair and one that starts with a very light breakfast. Most Spaniards eat a simple breakfast of toast or perhaps some spongy cookies or pastries with a cup of *café con leche* or coffee with milk (the Spanish equivalent of a Starbucks café latte).

Often a Spaniard will have a late morning snack, followed by a late and usually quite large lunch or *comida*, then a snack before a late but filling dinner or *cena*. Lunch is the biggest meal of the day and is often eaten about 2 P.M. Most stores close from 1 P.M. until 4 P.M. so Spaniards can relax and enjoy lunch. This was, in many years past, followed by a short period of rest or *siesta*. Then after 4 P.M., a Spaniard works for a few more hours before heading home and eating dinner quite late in the evening, around 10 P.M.

Where do tapas fit in? Tapas are often snacked upon between meals, especially between lunch and dinner.

But though the tapas tradition serves a practical, hunger-filling need, tapas are never just about the food. Tapas are about connecting with old and new friends and are embraced as part of the Spanish tradition of fully enjoying life's pleasures. Besides grabbing a nosh on the way home from work, a Spaniard will share the company of friends, jockey and joke with the waiter or bartender, and in general, just enjoy the social scene.

The tapas tradition is such a part of the Spanish culture that it has even inspired a new verb, *tapear*, which means to sample different tapas at different bars and restaurants.

> **Appetizing Extras**
>
> In the beginning, most tapas traditionally were served and eaten while standing, and many bars continue this tradition to this day.

> **Hablo Tapas**
>
> *Tapear* is the Spanish verb that means to visit different tapas establishments, and the *tapeo* is essentially a tapas pub crawl.

Culinary Regions of Spain

Sometimes, the Spanish refer to their country as *Las Espanas* or the Spains, in plural, because of the many different and so distinctive regions that make up their country.

Nineteen different regions divide Spain, and each region is subdivided further into provinces. Each little province has its own regional, culinary specialties. But, overall, the culinary specialties can be basically divided into seven different regions.

The North Coast, including Basque Country, Galicia and Cantabria, and Asturias, is known for its seafood and highly seasoned sauces. A good example of a tapas dish from this region would be seafood *empanadas* or filled pastries.

The Northeastern Interior, including Aragon and Rioja, is known for its vegetables, particularly its beans and peppers. A good example of a tapas dish from this region would be filled piquillo peppers, a special, small, sweet red pepper.

Catalonia is known for casseroles, garlic mayonnaise or alioli sauce, and Spanish sparkling wine or *cava*. Alioli sauce is often served with *patatas bravas* or fried potatoes served with a spicy sauce. The Balearic Islands (Ibiza, Majorca, and Menorca), though a distinct region of Spain, often are culinarily included with Catalonia. The Central and Western Interior, including Castillo-Leon, Castillo-La Mancha, and Extremadura, is a land of rolling wheat and high plains. The land of Don Quixote, it is known for its roasts, chorizo or sausage, and Manchego cheese, the most popular and well-known Spanish cheese in the world. *Tortilla Español* is a common tapas dish here, but it is also served throughout Spain.

The Levantian Coast, with its cities of Valencia and Murcia, is known for its rice and paella dishes.

Andalusia is known throughout the world for its sherries, its olives, and its gazpacho or chilled tomato soup. Olives are a very, very common tapas dish—whether served by themselves, stuffed with cheese or peppers, or specially marinated.

The Canary Islands are a world unto themselves, and these seven little islands in the Atlantic (off the coast of Africa) grow many tropical fruits and vegetables and are known for their *mojos* or uncooked sauces which are made with olive oil, vinegar, and different spices. Avocado is grown here and can be combined into tapas dishes.

The Least You Need to Know

◆ Spain's unique history and the convergence of different conquering peoples—the Moors, the Romans, etc.—left their influence on not only Spanish culture but also Spanish cuisine.

◆ Many legends tell about how the tapas tradition got started, but most likely Spanish bartenders started it.

◆ Tapas is a part of the Spanish style of eating and is not just about the food; it is also about socializing.

◆ Spain has seven different culinary regions, and each region has its own special tapas dishes.

Chapter 2

Stocking Your Spanish Pantry

In This Chapter

- ◆ Key ingredients for Spanish tapas
- ◆ Necessary equipment for cooking
- ◆ Basic cooking techniques and tricks of the trade

Ingredients, equipment, and technique, the three building blocks of all cuisines, are equally necessary for making tapas. The ingredients serve as the foundation of cuisine, while the right equipment and techniques make building the cuisine possible.

In this chapter, we explore the ingredients you need to create authentic tapas, the equipment your kitchen should be outfitted with, and a handful of tried and true cooking techniques that can make the job easier. This chapter helps you build your own Spanish *cocina* (kitchen).

Not So Secret ... Ingredients

The starting point for tapas is the ingredients. But before we even start talking about the actual foods, we need to emphasize quality. If you use superior ingredients, you'll end up with a stellar dish, but use mediocre ingredients, and you'll end up with less than stellar results. "You start with the best quality ingredients that are in season, and you go from there," says Chef Matt Silverman, executive chef for Agave and Vintner's Grill in Las Vegas.

While it is possible to ruin good ingredients, it is impossible to elevate lesser ingredients. This doesn't mean you have to blow your food budget on just one dish, but it does mean you should be discerning when you shop. For example, never buy greens that are already wilting, and always purchase meat and seafood as fresh as possible.

It is also worth noting that because Spanish cuisine does not often feature heavy, buttery or cream-laden sauces, the quality of the ingredients—good or bad—shines through.

"Gourmet cooking is all about using high-quality ingredients and implementing the proper techniques," says Jill Prescott, chef and founder of Jill Prescott's Cooking School, where she teaches the proper techniques to home cooks.

Three high-quality ingredients you want to use are heavy cream, unsalted butter, and sea salt or kosher salt. Heavy cream or cream with 40 percent milk fat does not contain any additives like guar gum, which means that when you heat it on the stove, it won't break down, and when you use it to top a dessert, it won't melt into a puddle.

Unsalted butter is preferable to salted butter because salt is only added to prolong a butter's shelf life at the grocery store. By using unsalted butter, you not only get fresher quality, but you can also better control the amount of salt in your dishes—they won't ever taste too salty.

Regular table salt just never quite tastes as good as sea salt or kosher salt. Sea salt is my personal salt of choice, and except for baking, the salt I use in everything. I also always choose one without the extra iodine because that imparts an off-flavor.

Tapas on Tap

The main ingredients for tapas are the same as for regular Spanish cuisine, the backbone of which includes olive oil, olives, garlic, and paprika. Other important ingredients include *jamon* or ham, saffron, and Marcona almonds.

In Spain, fresh produce, from greens to chickpeas, spinach to eggplant, is a high priority. Spaniards eat a lot of seafood, along with beef and chicken, but pork or *lomo* is extremely popular.

> ⌐**Hablo Tapas** ___
>
> *Lomo* is the Spanish word for pork tenderloin. Pork and ham are popular in Spain.

Love at First Press: Olive Oil

If a Spanish dish contains oil, it's olive oil. In fact, if there's a single, most important ingredient in Spanish cuisine, it would be olive oil, hands down. It is used for frying, sautéing, marinating, drizzling … if there's a use for olive oil, it's used.

Because Spain is the largest producer of olive oil in the world, it's not surprising that it plays such an important role in their food preparation. About 260 different farmers press their olives into oil, and most of these farmers live in Andalusia, which accounts for 80 percent of Spain's oil production.

The five kinds of olives most often pressed into oil include: picual (fruity and from Andalusia), arbequina (fruity and piquant and from Catalonia), picudo (fruity and from Andalusia), cornicabra (rustic and from Toledo, outside of Madrid), and jojiblanca (fruity, sometimes sweet, and from Cordoba).

Olive oil is made from a paste of crushed olives. The oil is separated from the paste when put through a machine that spins around; the centrifugal force generated by the machine separates the oil from the paste. This process is known as *cold pressing*.

> ⌐**Hablo Tapas** ___
>
> **Cold pressing** is an anachronistic term. Fifty years ago, before centrifugal machines were used, olive oil was made in vertical presses. The first press was called cold pressing. The paste was then mixed with hot water or steam and repressed; the resulting pressing or pressings were never as good as the first cold press because the heat treatment removed flavors. The first press is called extra-virgin.

Extra-virgin olive oil is the best pressing. It contains only 1 percent acidity whereas virgin olive oils can contain up to 2 percent acidity.

Extra-virgin and virgin olive oils are the best tasting olive oils and the only olive oils I cook with.

Other types of olive oil include: pure (also known as refined), light, and pomace. These oils are created by applying heat and chemicals when the olive paste is being pressed. Pure or refined olive oil is a blend of virgin olive oils with subsequent pressings; it is "refined" with charcoal and other filters. Light olive oil refers not to calorie content but to a lighter, less olive-oil-tasting oil. Pomace oil is created from the ground flesh and olive pits; this inferior quality oil is better for making soap than cooking.

While olive oil may be *the* oil to use in Spain, you might wonder how available Spanish olive oil is in the United States. Most grocery stores carry at least one brand of Spanish olive oil. Some good Spanish brands include Goya, Pompeian, Carbonell, and Star. Less common but exceedingly good brands include Zoe and *Las Brisas* organic olive oil. The King of Spanish Olive Oil is "Nunez de Prado." Generally considered the best, it comes from Andalusia.

> **Appetizing Extras**
>
> Even some olive oils labeled as Italian are actually made from Spanish olives; the olives are imported to Italy where they are pressed and blended.

Vampires Aren't of Spanish Legend: Garlic

If Spanish cuisine starts with olive oil, then it ends with garlic. In many Spanish dishes, there's no such thing as too much garlic. It's found in sauces, like alioli (sometimes spelled aioli) or garlic mayonnaise, in soup (garlic soup), in meats, and in vegetable dishes. It's rubbed on bread, used to marinate and stuff olives, and sprinkled in just about everything except desserts and drinks.

Most chefs recommend you peel and chop garlic before cooking, and in most of the tapas recipes in this book, the garlic should be *minced*.

> **Hablo Tapas**
>
> To **mince** means to finely chop something.

Most recipes require not one or two, but usually, several cloves of garlic. If you are pressed for time, use a garlic press or use a minced garlic preserved in olive oil. Another option is to buy frozen, minced garlic. A Spaniard wouldn't even think of using canned garlic. Another time-saver is to slice the garlic instead of chopping it.

Hot 'n' Spicy

The one thing you do *not* want to use is garlic powder or garlic salt. They are not an equal substitute for fresh garlic.

A Branch of Olives

As Spain is the world's largest producer of olive oil, it is also the world's largest cultivator of table olives, counting for a harvest of more than 725 million pounds every year. Olives are an ancient fruit native to the Mediterranean and grown for at least 5,000 years. The region of Andalusia in southern Spain is the largest producer of olives in Spain, accounting for 75 percent of all olives grown in the country. The other two main olive producing regions are Extremadura and Castille.

Manzanilla fina, small, green olives, and gordal, large, plump olives, are two of the most commonly exported varieties of Spanish olives to the United States. Arbequina, small, reddish-brown olives grown in Catalonia, are also growing on America's taste buds.

Olives, specially marinated or stuffed with delicacies like anchovies, peppers, or almonds, are a common, easy tapas, but olives are also added to many other dishes. They are chopped and stuffed in *empanadas* (filled pastries), tossed in salads, and added to meat dishes.

Appetizing Extras

Both olives and olive oil are a great source of monounsaturated fats—a healthy fat that does not raise your level of bad cholesterol (LDL) and can even increase your level of good cholesterol (HDL).

Sherry Wine and Sherry Wine Vinegar

Sherry wine and especially sherry wine vinegar are also important to Spanish cuisine. Sherry wine and sherry vinegar are produced in the Jerez or Sherry region of Andalusia in Spain. Though sherry wine is great to drink, it's also good to add to many tapas dishes because it kicks a sauce up another notch and lends a sweet, almost subtle flavoring to meats.

In Spanish cooking, sherry vinegar is even more important than straight sherry wine as it is used in vinaigrettes, marinades, and sauces. It is produced by a second fermentation of sherry wine in which the wine is packed in oak barrels where a bacteria converts the alcohol to acid. It ranges in color from light caramel to dark crimson, getting darker and richer in color as it ages.

Sherry wine vinegar has two different *Denominacion de Origen* (DO) or protected product statuses: *Vinaigre de Jerez* or Sherry Vinegar, which is aged for at least six months and *Vinaigre de Jerez Reserva* (Reserve Sherry Vinegar), which is aged for at least two years.

Appetizing Extras

Protected origin status of products is something countries in the European Union do to protect important products. These labels certify that food products have been made under stringent, high-quality circumstances in particular regions of a country. You can't, for example, get a Manchego cheese that's been made in the Netherlands.

It's Not Paprikash—Paprika

Pick a pack of peppers, and in Spain, most likely they'll be dried and ground into *pimenton* or paprika. Paprika is the most important spice in the Spanish spice drawer. They are picked and then smoked over white oak. Then they are ground into paprika. It comes from Extremadura in west central Spain right next to Portugal.

Paprika is made from dried, ground peppers, ranging from the mild red bell pepper to hot, hot chile peppers. About 50 percent of the paprika the United States imports comes from Spain, and most of the Spanish paprika you'll find is the *dulce* or sweet, mild version of Spanish paprika. There are also bittersweet or *agridulce* and hot or *picante* versions, each hotter than the *dulce* version.

But even the *dulce* version has a smoky tang to it and is hotter than say, a Hungarian paprika. In the recipes of this book, it is best to use a *dulce* paprika, but if you like things hot, you might want to try the *agridulce* or *picante* versions. Just keep in mind, the hotter the paprika, the less you want to use in your recipes.

Paprika is largely grown in the Vera region of Extremadura, near Murcia and has its own protection of origin designation.

The Expensive Taste of Saffron

As the world's most expensive spice, saffron typically costs upward of $500 per pound in bulk, with retail costs sometimes exceeding ten times that price. Fortunately, despite its incredible cost, most recipes only require a pinch or two—typically all that's inside the cellophane pouch in a "jar" of saffron.

As with olives and olive oil, Spain is one of the world's largest producer of this rare spice, cultivating more than 70 percent of the world's production. Introduced to Spain in the eighth century by the Moors, saffron is actually the dried stigmas of a crocus flower, and about 200 flowers are needed to produce just one gram of the spice. Most of Spain's saffron is grown on the high plains of La Mancha—the region in central Spain where Don Quixote hails from.

Saffron gives a golden hue and subtle flavor to dishes. In Spain, it is most commonly used in the seafood-rice dish of paella. But it can also be added to sauces, soups, breads, and even desserts, like flan. Saffron must be stored in an airtight container and kept in the dark.

Appetizing Extras

In Afghanistan, saffron is being looked at as a substitute crop for opium cultivation.

Jamon Hambone

Jamon or ham is an important food in Spain and an especially important ingredient for tapas. On the Iberian peninsula, pork and ham date back to Roman times, and Spanish ham is prized around the world for its delicious, rich flavors.

Not only that, but Spain is the largest producer of air-dried-cured ham in the world, and Spaniards eat more ham than anyone else on the planet.

Two main types of Spanish ham are available in the United States: Serrano ham or *jamon Serrano* and Iberian ham or *jamon Iberico*. *Jamon Serrano*, which translates roughly as mountain ham, is the most commonly found type. Cured for a period of 7 to 16 months, Serrano ham tastes a little bit similar to proscuitto, except it is leaner and has a more smoky taste.

Iberian ham, which is prized because the free-roaming hogs are fed almost exclusively on acorns, offers a nuttier, more depth of ham flavor. Cured for a period of two to three years, this expensive meat, which typically costs $100 per pound, became available in the United States only in late 2007.

> ### Appetizing Extras
>
> If you visit Spain, check out a *Museo de Jamon*, which translates to museum of ham. Not a museum but a restaurant, the *Museo de Jamon* is a great place to try different Spanish hams. They make an exceptionally good ham *croqueta* or fried fritter.

Simply Sausage: Chorizo

Almost as much as their beloved ham, Spaniards really do love their sausages. Spanish chorizo, sometimes shortened to the diminutive nickname of *chori*, is not the same as Mexican chorizo or Caribbean varieties.

> ### Appetizing Extras
>
> La Española Meats (www.laespanolameats.com) is a company in California that not only imports great Spanish sausages, but the company also makes fresh sausages using traditional Spanish recipes.

Many chorizos are flavored with paprika and garlic, and I would say, they are closer in taste to Italian or Portuguese sausages than Mexican varieties. Most imported Spanish sausages are the dry varieties, cured and ready-to-eat right out of the package. Some dry varieties include the paprika-laden Leon Herradura, the garlicky de Leon, and the salami-esque Pamplona.

There are also semicured, cooking varieties of chorizo, which include Bilbao, from the city of Bilbao, del Pireneo, from the Pyrenees, and de Teruel, from Aragon.

For tapas recipes that call for chorizo, use a dry or completely cured variety like Leon Herradura.

Saying Cheese and Other Spanish Delights

Spanish cheese is simply a delight! The most popularly imported Spanish cheese is Manchego, in all of its varieties from young to aged to organic. But Spain produces more than 100 different types of cheese, and dozens of Spanish cheeses are imported in the United States.

Manchego, made from sheep's milk, is the most important cheese to know. Other cheeses good for appetizers include Mahon, a cow's milk cheese made on the island of Minorca and the second most popular cheese in Spain; Iberico, a hard and crumbly cheese that is reminiscent of Parmesan; and Cabrales, Spain's most famous blue cheese.

Besides cheese, a good Spanish importer will sell everything from pickled asparagus to lemon bars, from Spanish mixed nuts to olive oil cracker cakes. Though you can use all of these imported delicacies in creating tapas, some foods are more important than others.

For sheer cooking value and distinctive flavoring, there are three Spanish foods you shouldn't substitute if at all possible: Spanish tuna, piquillo peppers, and Marcona almonds.

◆ Most of Spain's tuna, which comes packed in olive oil, is harvested from the Atlantic in the Galicia region of northwest Spain. For a special treat try ventresca tuna or the expensive, tuna belly. If you cannot find Spanish tuna for a recipe, substitute with Italian tuna or another oil-packed variety of tuna.

◆ Piquillo peppers are simply the sweetest, little red peppers I've ever tasted. Picked and roasted by hand in the Navarre region before being packed in jars, they are the perfect peppers to stuff and add a touch of sweetness to any dish. They can be substituted with roasted red peppers, but regular red peppers are about three times the size of a piquillo and aren't nearly as sweet or mild.

◆ Marcona almonds are larger and more flavorful than regular almonds and a real treat. If you can't find them, regular almonds are an adequate substitution. You can also use toasted hazelnuts to approximate the taste of Marconas.

Stocking Your Kitchen

If you have a well-stocked, regular kitchen, then you're ready to start making tapas. But in case you're wondering what a well-stocked kitchen contains, here is my starter recipe for a basic kitchen: a good pot, a good pan, a good knife, a mixing bowl, a whisk, measuring cups and spoons, and a wooden spoon. You can make everything in this book with just these pieces of equipment.

However, it's a lot easier if you have a few more things—like a really good set of pots and pans, a set of mixing bowls, or a set of knives. Beyond that, it is advantageous to have a good blender or food processor, ramekins or custard dishes for making flan, a vegetable peeler, a can opener, a sturdy garlic press that will crush unpeeled garlic cloves, a good roasting pan, cookie sheets, a fresh pepper grinder, and a *microplane* or specialty grater.

> **Hablo Tapas**
>
> A **microplane** is a new-fangled type of grater that makes it easier to grate cheese, chocolate, and spices. It also zests citrus fruits or removes the colored peel without the pith.

Technical Expertise

A little bit of know-how goes a long way in the kitchen, and knowing a few chef's secrets will make the cooking process much easier. Using the correct techniques will better enable you to achieve success.

Precooking Preambles

Before you sauté or fry something, always heat the pan first. If you heat the pan for a minute or two with nothing in it, then your dishes will cook more quickly and evenly. I usually heat the pan for a minute or two, add the oil for a minute or two, and then add my ingredients.

It is equally important to preheat the oven. When baking or roasting dishes in the oven, it's also important to know exact temperatures. Because some ovens, especially older ones, do not always heat temperatures to the exact degree shown on the dial, it's a good idea to purchase an oven thermometer. However, you can use any cooking thermometer to check your oven's temperature. Just heat your oven, and put the ther-mometer on a pan for a minute. Remove using oven mitts, and see if the temperature on the oven matches the reading on the thermometer. If it's too low or too high, then adjust accordingly.

Keep them Separated

Separating an egg is pretty basic. Many people just crack the shell on a hard surface and carefully divide the egg over a bowl, letting some of the white drip into the bowl, gently moving the yolk from one shell to the other to drain the white, and then dropping the yolk into a separate bowl.

But sometimes the yolk may break or a bit of shell may get into a bowl. That's why it's always a good idea to crack the eggs individually into a bowl and put the perfectly divided whites and yolks into separate bowls. If you crack an egg over a bowl of whites and the yolk breaks, you might have to start all over again.

Tapas Tricks

If just a bit of yolk or shell gets into the bowl, use a larger bit of shell to scoop it. The yolk and/or shell pieces will be attracted to the larger shell like a magnet.

A Perfect Cut

When cutting fruits, vegetables, or meats, it's most imperative to use a sharpened knife. Not only will it be easier to cut, dice, or chop, but it is also safer. You are less likely to cut yourself by using a sharp knife than using a dull one. Also curl your fingers under so you don't chop them.

Some vegetables, like onions, tend to be more of a chore to chop—and not only because they make you cry. One way to speed up the dicing process is to first cut the onion in half, right through the root end. Score the half both vertically and horizontally, slicing lengthwise and crosswise but not quite cutting all the way through. Then simply slice through as if you were going to cut slices, and the onion will fall apart into little diced pieces. This technique can also be used on garlic cloves and shallots.

Into the Frying Pan

A lot of Spanish tapas dishes are fried, and in Spain the only oil used is olive oil. Olive oil does not have as high a smoking temperature—the temperature to which you can heat it before it burns or smokes in the pan—as some oils, like corn or canola. If cost is an issue use a good canola oil and then drizzle a little extra-virgin on the dish after it is done cooking.

Don't heat olive oil beyond 355°F—its smoking point. To see how hot the oil is, use a cooking thermometer, or cut a small piece of bread and drop it into the oil. If the bread turns golden within a minute's time, then the oil is ready to fry.

Tapas Tricks

After frying, you can reuse olive oil up to four times if you cool it and then drain it through a cheesecloth or clean paper towels over a colander.

Although a good rule of thumb is to heat the pan first, heating oil is an exception to that rule. Put the oil in the pan, and then heat it up. Also, do not crowd the pan. Too many pieces of food lower the temperature, which means your food will take longer to cook and most likely get soggy.

The Least You Need to Know

◆ The two most important ingredients in Spanish cuisine are extra-virgin olive oil and garlic.

◆ Other key ingredients include sherry wine and sherry wine vinegar, olives, paprika, saffron, ham, chorizo, and cheese.

◆ A well-stocked regular kitchen is perfectly suited to making tapas.

◆ Knowing a few culinary techniques will make cooking tapas a breeze.

Part 2

Cold Tapas

Most Spanish restaurants divide their tapas offerings into two sections, cold and hot. This part covers the cold stuff. That doesn't mean the tapas are uncooked; it simply means that all the sauces, sandwiches, vegetables, potatoes, egg, meat, and seafood dishes are best enjoyed with a little chill to them. But some of these dishes you can also enjoy hot. (My husband—bless his heart—always warms his gazpacho in the microwave.) This part also includes some simple, quick, and easy dishes to get you started.

3

Fast and Easy: Simple Tapas

In This Chapter

- ◆ Pop and serve favorites
- ◆ Cheese and ham plates
- ◆ Simple sauces
- ◆ Little bites and mini sandwiches

Sometimes you can make the easiest tapas with just a can opener and a food processor, and sometimes it's even simpler than that. In fact, these tapas are in the same genre as what were most likely the very first tapas ever served: simple pieces of bread, topped with little bits of cheese or other goodies.

Put together a little dish of olives or almonds, some good bread, and a cheese or cheese and ham plate, and you have tapas. Add a few relatively easy, no-cook sauces, and you've kicked it up a notch without adding too much work. And if you include a salad, a good bottle of wine, and a purchased dessert from the grocery, then you can invite the neighbors over for a quick tapas dinner.

These dishes, while delicious enough by themselves, can be added to other tapas to augment a tapas dinner or to just provide a simple yet elegant start to another meal. They are also great dishes to make when you need something for a potluck meal or event.

The sauces in this chapter also serve as the basis of flavor for more complicated dishes in other chapters—homemade mayonnaise, for example, serves as the foundation for *huevos rellenos* or Spain's gourmet answer to Aunt Marge's famous deviled eggs.

This chapter not only introduces you to the simple ways of making tapas but also explains the use of some of the standard flavors of Spain—olives, piquillo peppers, and paprika. Simplicity serves as the foundation for all the foods and recipes in this chapter, making it a great place to start cooking on your tapas journey.

Pop and Serve

Whether I'm making a simple, quick summer tapas dinner for just my husband and me or entertaining for 50, I always include some pop-and-serve tapas basics. As the name implies, these are the plated or dished varieties of tapas, and a good gourmet grocery store—either in your own town or online—should be able to get you jars, tins, or plastic-wrapped versions of these goodies.

Perhaps the most ubiquitous of the pop-and-serve variety is the olive. In Spain, practically every bar and tapas joint has them on hand. Olives are to Spanish bars what peanuts used to be to American bars. The three main olives to munch on are arbequina olives from Cataluna, empeltre olives from Aragon, and manzanilla olives from Andalusia. You can buy these types of olives individually, and many stores carry jars with a mix of all three.

Olives also come stuffed with jalapeños, garlic, peppers, and more, or marinated in paprika and other spices. In some places in Spain, the proprietors will marinate mixed olives with crushed garlic, sherry vinegar, orange or lemon juice, extra-virgin olive oil, and spices.

Olives aren't the only from jar to dish appetizers. Marcona almonds are another quick and easy appetizer. These Spanish nuts are known for their sweetness and soft, cashew-like texture. In Spain, they are hand-picked and hand-fried in small batches. That means you really don't have to toast them. While you can use them in classical Spanish dishes, they make an ideal tapas all by themselves, and you can also add them to accent Spanish cheese or Spanish cheese and ham plates.

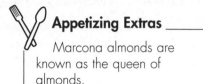

Appetizing Extras

Marcona almonds are known as the queen of almonds.

Another good tapas, right out of the jar, are piquillo peppers. These red peppers are so sweet—yet firm. They are great by themselves in a pretty little dish sprinkled with fresh parsley or cilantro, or you can dice or cut them into little strips and add them as garnish to practically any tapas dish.

Queso and *Jamon*

Manchego cheese and Serrano ham go together like peanut butter and jelly. Very often, they are served on a plate together, perhaps with a few olives in the center. Just buy thinly sliced Serrano or Iberian ham and then sliver some Manchego, and you're good to go.

Manchego and Serrano also sometimes top another simple tapas—*pan con tomate*, in which tomato is rubbed onto toasted bread.

Tapas Tricks

Artisanal or aged Manchego has more flavor than young Manchego, but if you want the cheese to have more perfect slices, then go with a young Manchego.

If you are a vegetarian—or don't like ham—you can eat Manchego or other Spanish cheeses plain or together on a cheese plate. Spain makes more than 100 different and distinct cheeses, but you don't need that many to make a good cheese plate. In fact, I recommend no more than four to six cheeses for a Spanish cheese tasting. Count on about 2 ounces of cheese per person, and arrange the cheeses, whole, not sliced on a platter.

Besides Manchego, good cheeses to try include: Mahon, Drunken Goat (goat cheese soaked in red wine), Iberico, Garrotxa, San Simon, and Cabrales.

Some traditional Spanish accompaniments to cheese include: quince paste, Marcona almonds, date and almond cakes or bars, fig and almond cakes or bars, and olive oil crisps, sugared or savory.

Mayonesas

One of the basic building blocks for several Spanish tapas is a good, homemade mayonnaise or *mayonesa*, and this chapter contains recipes for this foundation sauce as well as three variations.

Homemade mayonnaise tastes better than any store bought version, and it requires few ingredients. The basis is egg yolks with extra-virgin olive oil whisked in. Because you are using uncooked egg yolks, it is extremely important to use either local, organic eggs of a very high quality or pasteurized eggs. That way, you will not get food poisoning from the uncooked yolks.

Homemade mayonnaise is often served with bread and as a dip for many different tapas.

Little Bits and Bites

Little bits of food impaled on toothpicks or skewers are always fun, and in Spain, these are known as *banderillas.* These yummy bites are sort of mix and match treats. Use meats, cheeses, and seafood, and add marinated vegetables and perhaps a drizzle of Spanish olive oil or sherry vinegar. You can also call them *pinchos* (in Catalan) or *pintxos* (in Basque).

For example, try a piece or two of Manchego, skewered with a fig or a square of quince paste. Or put Manchego and ham together on a skewer. Take a piece of chorizo with a piece of Manchego or Cabrales.

> **Hablo Tapas**
>
> *Banderillas* are little bits of food, skewered on tooth-picks. Their name comes from the colorful swords used by *banderillos* to weaken the bulls before the *matadores* come in to kill them.

Match a small shrimp with some piquillo peppers. Or take a chunk of smoked or poached salmon, sandwiched between slices of cucumber or pickles. Try a small piece of chicken with a piece of marinated artichoke heart and a piquillo pepper. Or just pair the chicken up with some cheese.

Basically, the combinations are endless—limited only by your imagination or what you have in your cupboard. And dip your *banderillas* in a trio of homemade *mayonesas* or some extra-virgin olive oil.

Use long and short skewers or toothpicks, and stack the skewers with two to about four pieces of food. For artistic arrangement, stake them in a cutout piece of cardboard or foam or on a pineapple. Arrange them simply on a plate, or put them in shot glasses.

Bocadillas or Spanish Sandwiches

Most *bocadillas* or Spanish sandwiches can be consumed as a meal, on the go, but they can also be transformed into wonderful little appetizers. As with *banderillas*, *bocadillas* are limited only by your imagination.

Marinated Olives

Plenty of upscale grocery stores sell olives marinated in a variety of spices, but they usually don't taste as good as those flavored with a homemade marinade.

1 orange, zest and juice

1 lemon, zest and juice

½ cup extra-virgin olive oil

4 to 6 cloves garlic, minced

4 TB. sherry wine vinegar

1 to 2 tsp. Spanish paprika

1 to 2 tsp. cumin

2 cups mixed olives of your choice

> **Yield: About 2 cups**
>
> **Prep Time:** 5 minutes
>
> **Marinate Time:**
> Overnight or one week
>
> **Serving Size:** ¼ cup

1. In a large bowl, mix together orange zest, orange juice, lemon zest, lemon juice, olive oil, garlic, vinegar, and spices. Mix in olives.

2. Let stand, covered overnight, or refrigerate for up to a week. Serve with marinade.

 Tapas Tricks

Serve olives and their marinade with crusty bread as the marinade tastes delicious when sopped up.

Olive Tapenade

The French and Italians aren't the only ones to chop up olives and serve them on toast.

4 oz. pitted kalamata or other black olives

2 TB. extra-virgin olive oil

1 TB. sherry wine vinegar

1 tsp. *capers*

> **Yield: About ¾ cup**
>
> **Prep Time:** 5 minutes
>
> **Serving Size:** About 2 tablespoons

1. Place olives, olive oil, vinegar, and capers into a food processor fitted with a standard chopping blade. Chop 2 to 3 minutes or until finely minced.

2. Serve with crackers or crusty bread.

Variation: Chopped tomatoes, basil, parsley, or even preserved lemons can also be added to your tapenade.

Hablo Tapas

Though olives form the base of *tapenade,* the word *tapenade* comes from the Provençal word *tapeno,* which means capers. **Capers** are actually the buds of a Mediterranean flower preserved in vinegar. They offer a delicious tang to dishes.

Creamy Olive Tapenade

For some people, the taste of tapenade is a little too intense. The cheese and crème fraîche lightens yet complements the olive taste.

1 batch Olive *Tapenade* (recipe earlier in this chapter)

3 oz. feta or Spanish goat cheese

2 oz. crème fraîche or cream cheese

Yield: About 1½ cups
Prep Time: 5 minutes
Serving Size: ¼ cup

1. Place tapenade, cheese, and crème fraîche into a food processor fitted with a standard blade. Chop 2 to 3 minutes or until finely mixed.

2. Serve with crackers or crusty bread.

Tapas Tricks

For individual tapas dishes, try stuffing little cherry tomatoes with this creamy *tapenade* and topping it with just a touch of chopped fresh herbs, like parsley or dill.

Stuffed Piquillos

This dish is so simple yet tastes so good—so sweet and tart—you won't be able to stop at just one.

12 piquillo peppers

4 to 6 oz. fresh chèvre

Yield: 12 stuffed peppers
Prep Time: 10 minutes or less
Serving Size: 3 stuffed peppers

1. Holding pepper in hand, gently prop it open, and place 1 to 2 teaspoons chèvre inside. Repeat with all peppers.

Tapas Tricks

Until you get the hang of stuffing peppers, it can feel a bit awkward. Keep the hand that holds the peppers clean—otherwise it is easy to smear goat cheese on the outside of the peppers. That doesn't ruin the taste, but the tapas are not quite as appealing.

Variation: Inspired by a dish called "Red Pepper Ravioli" at the Restaurant Divino in Segovia, add one tsp. vanilla, 1 TB. honey, and 1 TB. milk to the goat cheese. Slice the peppers halfway on one side, then fill with 1 to 2 tsp. of the goat cheese. Place the peppers, slit side down on a plate, then fold the cut edges out so that the peppers appear to be folded pasta triangles.

Baked Goat Cheese with Piquillo Sauce

Instead of using a straight tomato sauce, I use chopped up piquillo peppers.

6 piquillo peppers or small, roasted red peppers with seeds and ribs removed

6 sun-dried tomatoes

½ cup yellow or white onion, roughly chopped

4 TB. red wine

2 TB. extra-virgin olive oil

2 cloves garlic, minced

¼ tsp. Spanish paprika

⅛ tsp. dried oregano

4 oz. log fresh chèvre

Yield: 4 to 6 servings

Prep Time: 5 minutes

Cook Time: 10 minutes

Serving Size: About 3 tablespoons sauce plus 1 oz. melted chèvre

1. Preheat broiler on high.

2. Put peppers, tomatoes, onion, wine, oil, garlic, paprika, and oregano into a food processor fitted with a standard chopping blade. Mince into smooth yet thick paste.

3. Pour paste into a shallow, ovenproof casserole dish, and set chèvre log in the middle of the dish.

4. Broil for 10 minutes or until sauce is bubbly and cheese is browned and melted. Serve with crusty bread or crackers.

Tapas Tricks

To vary the flavors of this dish, you can also use different cheeses. Try feta, blue, or a combination of cheeses.

Sherry Soaked Sultanas

Though this isn't traditionally served with Spanish cheeses, Spanish ingredients inspired it. I was introduced to this delicacy on a trip to visit California creameries.

1 cup golden or sultana raisins

²/₃ cup sweet or cream sherry

12 oz. Cabrales, Manchego, or another flavorful cheese

Yield: 1 cup
Prep Time: 1 minute
Marinate Time: 1 day
Serving Size: 1 to 2 tablespoons

1. In a bowl, mix together raisins and sherry. Cover and chill overnight.

2. To serve, spoon over thin slices or chunks of cheese.

Appetizing Extras

In medieval times, Spain exported its raisins to England, where they were considered quite the delicacy.

Pan con Tomate

This is Spain's answer to garlic bread—toasted bread rubbed with tomato pulp. You can enjoy this plain, serve it with dipping sauces, or use it as the basis for Manchego and *jamon* sandwiches.

2 large garlic cloves

12 thin slices baguette or crusty bread

¼ cup extra-virgin olive oil

1 medium and juicy tomato, cut in half

⅛ tsp. Kosher or sea salt or to taste

Yield: 12 slices
Prep Time: 5 minutes
Cook Time: 4 minutes
Serving Size: 3 slices

1. Preheat broiler or grill.

2. Rub garlic cloves over both sides of each piece of bread. Dip or brush each slice in olive oil.

3. Grill or broil 1 to 2 minutes on each side.

4. Rub one side of each bread piece with tomato half. Sprinkle with salt. Serve plain or with sauces.

 Appetizing Extras

This is a traditional dish in Cataluna, where it is known as *pa amb tomaquet,* and purists do not rub the bread with garlic. Others, like myself, think almost everything tastes better with garlic.

Mayonesa

Making this dressing takes a bit of effort, but you won't ever want to go back to the jarred kind after you've made this delicious sauce.

3 egg yolks

2½ cups extra-virgin olive oil or a canola olive oil blend

1 TB. freshly squeezed lemon juice

1 TB. Dijon mustard

¼ tsp. Kosher or sea salt

Fresh cracked white pepper

Yield: 2 cups
Prep Time: 15 to 20 minutes
Serving Size: 1 to 2 tablespoons

1. Whisk egg yolks together until light, about two minutes.

2. Add tiny drizzle of olive oil. Whisk until well blended, 1 to 2 minutes. Add another drizzle of olive oil. Whisk until well blended.

3. Keep whisking and drizzling very slowly so the yolks and olive oil emulsify together. Mixture will gradually thicken and become more pastelike.

4. After olive oil is completely blended, add lemon juice, mustard, salt, and pepper. Use immediately or chill.

Hot 'n' Spicy

You must drizzle only a little olive oil at a time, a few drops, and then whisk and repeat. This is of paramount importance—otherwise you will end up with a yolky, oily mess. It is very easy to add too much, so do not get distracted, or you'll have to start all over again. Also if the sauce starts to look "oily" add a tablespoon or two of water; this will help the emulsification.

Variation: For **Lemon *Mayonesa*,** take ½ cup homemade *mayonesa* and add juice and zest of ½ lemon. Serve immediately or chill. This is a perfect dipping sauce for poultry and seafood.

Alioli or Garlic Mayonnaise

This quintessential tapas sauce goes with bread or with potatoes ... it goes with practically anything. This sauce, in France and other countries, is called aioli.

½ cup homemade *mayonesa*

1 clove garlic, minced

1½ tsp. freshly squeezed lemon juice

1 TB. Dijon mustard

Yield: ½ cup
Prep Time: 5 minutes
Serving Size: 1 tablespoon

1. Whisk together *mayonesa*, garlic, lemon juice, and mustard.
2. Serve immediately or chill.

Appetizing Extras

If you think emulsifying egg yolks with olive oil is hard, try emulsifying olive oil with mashed-up garlic cloves. That was the more traditional way of making alioli or allioli, as it is sometimes spelled. Also, classically potatoes were used instead of egg to make alioli, the starch acting as the emulsifier.

Salsa Rosa

This is a perfect accompaniment to *tortilla Español*.

½ cup homemade *mayonesa*

1 TB. tomato sauce

¼ tsp. Spanish paprika

Yield: ½ cup
Prep Time: 5 minutes
Serving Size: 1 to 2 tablespoons

1. Whisk *mayonesa*, tomato sauce, and paprika together.

2. Serve immediately or chill.

Tapas Tricks

If you're pressed for time or don't enjoy making homemade *mayonesa*, the best store-bought substitute, which many chefs use, is Hellmann's.

Basic Banderillas de Queso

This is the perfect finger food tapas dish.

3 oz. feta

3 oz. young Manchego

2 oz. cooked chicken breast

3 oz. *quince paste*

> **Yield: About 3 dozen**
>
> **Prep Time:** 15 minutes
>
> **Serving Size:** 4 to 6 *banderillas*

1. Cut feta, Manchego, and chicken into small cubes.

2. Skewer—mix and match ingredients—with toothpicks and serve.

Hablo Tapas

Quince, known as *membrillo* in Spanish, is a common Spanish fruit, sort of like a cross between an apple and a pear. **Quince paste** is the boiled-down fruit, which comes in jellied blocks.

Bocadillas de Queso y Jamon

Slices of baguettes are great to use, but also use small, appetizer-size rolls.
These are great finger foods.

¹/₄ cup homemade *mayonesa*

1 batch *Pan con Tomate* (recipe in this
chapter)

12 thin slices Serrano ham

6 piquillo peppers, sliced in half

3 oz. Manchego, divided into 12 slices

Yield: 6 sandwiches
Prep Time: 15 minutes
Serving Size: 1 sandwich

1. Spread homemade *mayonesa* on bread. Add pepper, ham, and cheese.
   Garnish with fresh parsley.

Variation: For vegetarian friends, substitute avocados or spinach for the
ham.

Chapter 4

De La Tierra: From the Earth

In This Chapter

- ◆ Salads
- ◆ Salad dressings
- ◆ Other cold vegetable tapas

For some reason, Spain is not known as a land of vegetables. The reality, however, is that *legumbres* (Spanish word for vegetables) are an important part of Spanish cuisine and, most definitely, are an important part of tapas.

As Spaniards espouse a distinctly Mediterranean diet, vegetables play an important role. In fact, on the menus of many Spanish restaurants, vegetables have their own special category; they're not just side dishes meant to accent meat or seafood.

This chapter explores the art of making cold vegetable tapas. From the marinated carrots of Andalusia with their Moorish undertones of flavor, to a hearty, Spanish chef salad, you can serve these dishes on their own.

Orange and Mixed Greens Salad with Orange-Sherry Vinaigrette

This is the perfect salad; simple and delicious, it has earned rave reviews from my guests.

1 orange, zest and juice

¼ cup extra-virgin olive oil

1 TB. sherry wine vinegar

1 tsp. Dijon mustard

⅛ tsp. Kosher or sea salt

Freshly ground pepper

4 cups mixed greens

½ cup julienned red peppers

¼ diced red onion

¼ cup shredded carrot

¼ cup chopped, pitted olives like kalamatas

2 navel oranges, pith and rind removed and divided into segments

Yield: **4 servings**
Prep Time: 15 minutes
Serving Size: 1½ cups

1. Mix orange zest and juice, olive oil, vinegar, mustard, salt, and pepper in a food processor or blender.

2. In a bowl, toss together greens, peppers, onion, carrots, olives, oranges, and dressing. Serve immediately.

Variation: For some extra zip, add just a few tablespoons crumbled blue cheese like Cabrales or Gorgonzola. That takes this delicious salad to a new height.

Tapas Tricks

Though you can whisk together any vinaigrette, using a blender or food processor helps emulsify the oil and the vinegar, making it a smoother, richer dressing, says Matt Silverman, executive chef of Vintner's Grill and Agave restaurants in Las Vegas. This simple technique will distinguish your salad dressings.

Simple Sherry Vinaigrette

Although many Spanish salad dressings are only olive oil and a little vinegar, this vinaigrette is a slightly fancier, but an equally simple dressing.

$\frac{1}{2}$ cup extra-virgin olive oil

$\frac{1}{4}$ to $\frac{1}{3}$ cup sherry or white wine vinegar

1 TB. shallots, finely diced

1 tsp. Dijon mustard

$\frac{1}{8}$ tsp. sea salt

Freshly ground pepper

Yield: 1 cup
Prep Time: 5 minutes
Serving Size: About 2 to 3 tablespoons

1. Whisk together olive oil, sherry or vinegar, shallots, mustard, salt, and pepper in a bowl, or use a food processor or blender to combine ingredients.

Roasted Red Pepper and Caramelized Onion Salad

The combination of roasted and caramelized vegetables brings a sweet touch to any table.

2 red peppers, seeded, cored, and halved

1 green pepper, seeded, cored, and halved

1 tsp. extra-virgin olive oil

$\frac{1}{2}$ cup yellow or white onion, diced

1 batch Simple Sherry Vinaigrette (recipe in this chapter)

Yield: 2 cups
Prep Time: 30 minutes or less
Cook Time: 10 minutes
Serving Size: $\frac{1}{2}$ cup

1. Preheat broiler. Lay pepper halves on cookie sheet and broil for 10 minutes.

2. When pepper skins are bubbly and mostly blackened, remove from oven. Place in a paper bag and cool for 10 minutes.

3. Heat skillet over medium-high heat for 1 minute. Add oil and heat for 1 minute. Add onion and sauté until caramelized, about 5 minutes. Remove from heat.

4. Slice peppers into thin, long slices.

5. Toss peppers, onion, and dressing together in a bowl. Serve by itself or over greens.

Tapas Tricks _____

If you are pressed for time, use canned, roasted red peppers, but they won't taste quite as fresh or sweet. Unless you are using piquillos.

Orange, Artichoke, and Avocado Salad

This is a pretty salad, which you can dress with the Orange-Sherry Vinaigrette or the Simple Sherry Vinaigrette.

4 cups mixed greens

2 oranges, seeded, pith and peel removed, and cut into segments

2 avocados, seeded, peeled, and sliced into ¼ inch slices

8 oz. or 1 container pickled artichoke hearts

¼ cup red onion, thinly sliced

1 batch Orange-Sherry Vinaigrette or Simple Sherry Vinaigrette (recipe in this chapter)

Yield: 4 servings
Prep Time: 15 minutes
Serving Size: 1 cup mixed greens plus

1. Arrange 1 cup greens per plate.

2. Divide oranges, avocados, artichokes, and onion into four equal portions.

3. Alternate orange, avocado, and artichoke in a circle radiating from center of plated greens. Add onion in between for color.

4. Drizzle with 1 or 2 tablespoons dressing. Serve immediately.

Tapas Tricks

For variety, use blood oranges instead of regular oranges. Blood oranges are sweet, dark pink oranges that are at their peak in January or February. They are a bit more astringent than regular navel oranges, but they are quite delicious, and they offer a different color.

Spanish Chef Salad

Forget the julienned strips of ham and cheese. This version kicks a chef salad up a notch. Serve it as a tapas dish, or serve it in larger bowls, and it makes a good meal.

3 hard-boiled eggs, chopped

12 stalks pickled asparagus, diced

$\frac{1}{2}$ cup pickled mushrooms, halved

4 piquillo peppers, diced

$\frac{1}{2}$ cup pitted olives like kalamatas, diced

6 slices Serrano ham, diced

4 cups mixed greens

1 cup *Salsa Rosa* (recipe in Chapter 3)

4 TB. grated cheese like Manchego

Freshly grated pepper

Yield: 4 to 8 servings
Prep Time: 15 to 20 minutes
Serving Size: About 1$\frac{3}{4}$ cups

1. Toss eggs, asparagus, mushrooms, peppers, olives, and ham together.

2. Divide greens into serving bowls, and top with either $\frac{1}{4}$ or $\frac{1}{8}$ cup vegetables, ham, and egg. Divide dressing among servings. Top with

cheese, and serve with pepper. A serving size is about 1 cup greens topped with $1/4$ mixed vegetables or $1/2$ cup greens topped with $1/8$ mixed vegetables.

> **Appetizing Extras** _____
>
> In Spain, most regular salads—*ensalada mixta*—have bits of meat, cheese, and vegetables in them. Some turn out to be delicious; others seem to be made of kitchen leftovers.

Asparagus with Two Sauces

Nothing tastes quite like spring or early summer as asparagus does. This is a quick and easy tapas dish.

1 lb. fresh asparagus, stalk ends trimmed

1 batch Alioli Sauce (recipe in Chapter 3)

1 batch *Salsa Rosa* (recipe in Chapter 3)

$1/8$ tsp. Kosher or sea salt

Freshly ground pepper

Yield: About 12 spears

Prep Time: 5 minutes

Cook Time: 2 minutes

Serving Size: About 3 spears

1. Bring water in a large pot to boil. Blanche asparagus for 1 minute. Drain and cool in ice water.

2. Arrange asparagus on individual plates or serving platter. Serve immediately, or chill in refrigerator. Serve with Alioli and *Salsa Rosa*, salt, and pepper.

> **Hot 'n' Spicy** _____
>
> **Blanching** is a cooking technique in which vegetables, usually, are plunged into boiling water, removed after a short cooking period, and immediately dunked into ice water to stop the cooking process. Besides asparagus, this method is ideal for cooking green beans, broccoli, and even spinach, but you blanche spinach for a period of seconds, not minutes. This technique is also good for removing skins of tomatoes.

Baked Asparagus

Nothing tastes quite like spring or early summer as asparagus does. This is a quick and easy tapas dish.

1 lb. fresh asparagus, stalk ends trimmed

1 TB. extra-virgin olive oil

1 TB. sherry or balsamic vinegar

⅛ tsp. Kosher or sea salt

Freshly ground pepper

Yield: About 12 spears
Prep Time: 5 minutes
Cook Time: 10 to 15 minutes
Serving Size: About 3 spears

1. Preheat oven to 350°F.
2. Drizzle asparagus with olive oil, vinegar, salt, and pepper. Arrange on baking sheet. Bake for 10 to 15 minutes. Arrange asparagus on individual plates or serving platter. Serve immediately, or chill in refrigerator. Serve with Alioli and *Salsa Rosa*, salt, and pepper.

Appetizing Extras

If you are trying to cut calories, eliminate the olive oil, and just use the vinegar for flavoring.

Stuffed Asparagus with Two Sauces

This is an exceptional appetizer any time of the year, but it is especially delightful in spring when asparagus is in season. The saltiness of the salmon contrasts beautifully with the creaminess of the cheese and the crisp bite of asparagus.

1 batch Asparagus with Two Sauces (recipe in this chapter)

3 ounces cream cheese, softened

12 slices smoked salmon

Yield: 12 spears
Prep Time: 15 minutes
Serving Size: 3 spears

1. Prepare asparagus using above recipe.

2. Spread thin layer of cream cheese on each slice of salmon. Wrap covered slices around asparagus.

3. Chill and serve plain or with sauces.

Variation: For variety, instead of smoked salmon, use Serrano ham, or instead of cream cheese, use a spreadable chèvre or Boursin cheese.

Marinated Carrots

This is a popular tapas dish in Andalusia. Though ginger is not commonly added, it gives this dish a little extra kick.

3 cloves garlic, minced

3 TB. extra-virgin olive oil

2 TB. fresh squeezed orange juice

2 TB. sherry wine vinegar

1 orange, zest

2 tsp. freshly grated ginger

1 tsp. cumin

Salt and pepper

Fresh parsley, chopped (optional)

4 cups carrots, diced and cooked until tender

Yield: About 4 cups carrots
Prep Time: 5 minutes
Cook Time: 10 minutes
Marinate Time: At least 1 hour
Serving Size: About $^{1}/_{4}$ cup

1. Whisk together garlic, olive oil, orange juice, vinegar, orange zest, ginger, cumin, salt, pepper, and parsley (if using).

2. Steam carrots for 10 minutes. Toss marinade with carrots. Marinate at least 1 hour, preferably 1 day before serving. Add parsley just before serving.

Tapas Tricks

For dramatic flair, serve in individual shot glasses with sprigs of parsley or chives sticking out.

Curried Carrot Dip

This is a great dish to make with some leftover marinated carrots and is a completely vegan dish.

3 cups Marinated Carrots (recipe in this chapter)

2 TB. extra-virgin olive oil

2 tsp. freshly squeezed lemon juice

2 tsp. curry powder

Pinch cayenne or Spanish paprika

Yield: About 1½ cups dip
Prep Time: 5 minutes
Serving Size: About ¼ cup

1. Place carrots, olive oil, lemon juice, curry powder, and cayenne into a food processor fitted with a standard chopping blade. Chop for 3 minutes or until puréed.

2. Serve with crackers or crusty bread.

Variation: For individual canapés, spread about a tablespoon of purée over toasted baguette slices and sprinkle with a little chopped parsley.

Caramelized Onion Dip and Crudités

Forget those packages of onion soup mixed with sour cream. For crudités platters, nothing tastes better than homemade caramelized onion dip.

2 TB. extra-virgin olive oil

1 large yellow or white onion, diced

2 cups crème fraîche or sour cream

Salt and white pepper

4 cups cut-up vegetables, peppers, carrots, celery, etc.

Yield: 2 cups dip
Prep Time: 5 minutes
Cook Time: 10 minutes
Serving Size: ¼ cup dip plus vegetables or chips

1. Heat a medium-size pot over medium-high heat for 1 to 2 minutes. Add olive oil, and heat for 1 minute.

2. Add onion; sauté 5 to 10 minutes or until caramelized.

3. Remove from heat. Put onion, crème fraîche, salt, and pepper into a blender or food processor fitted with a standard chopping blade, and chop until smooth or about 5 minutes.

4. Serve with crudités or chips.

Variation: For a little extra flavor, add two tablespoons grated cheese like Parmesan or Manchego.

 Tapas Tricks

> You can cook this longer for up to about 30-40 minutes over low heat to get a good deep brown color. You can also use a small amount of water to deglaze the pan (a tablespoon or two at a time).

Gazpacho

As perhaps the most well-known dish from Andalusia, this cold soup is like a liquid, refreshing salad.

2 cups tomato juice

1 cup dried breadcrumbs

2 cups Roma tomatoes, cored, seeded, and diced

1 cup white or yellow onion, diced

1 cup cucumber, peeled, seeded, and diced

½ cup red pepper, cored, seeded, and diced

1 jalapeño pepper, cored, seeded, and diced

¼ cup cilantro or parsley, finely chopped

8 cloves garlic, minced

¼ cup extra-virgin olive oil

⅛ cup sherry wine vinegar

½ tsp. Kosher or sea salt

Freshly ground pepper

Yield: About 8 cups
Prep Time: 20 minutes
Marinate Time: At least 1 hour
Serving Size: ½ cup

1. Place tomato juice and breadcrumbs into a food processor fitted with a standard blade. Chop 2 to 3 minutes or until finely mixed.

2. Mix tomatoes, onion, cucumber, red pepper, jalapeño, cilantro, and garlic together. Add olive oil, vinegar, salt, and pepper.

3. Add juice-bread purée to vegetable mix.

4. Return mixture to the food processor in 2-cup portions. Chop 2 to 3 minutes or until mixture is somewhat chunky.

4. Marinate for at least 1 hour before serving.

Appetizing Extras

Though Americans may associate gazpacho with tomatoes, the foundation of the soup is actually the breadcrumbs, which give this cold dish a more creamy texture, making it not just a lumpy glass of V-8.

Quick and Dirty Gazpacho

If you're pressed for time, try this tasty alternative to dicing vegetable upon vegetable.

2 cups tomato juice

1 cup dried breadcrumbs

4 cups fresh or quality-jarred mild salsa

¼ fresh cilantro or parsley, finely chopped

⅛ tsp. Kosher or sea salt

Freshly ground pepper

Yield: About 6 cups
Prep Time: 20 minutes
Marinate Time: At least 1 hour
Serving Size: ½ cup

1. Place tomato juice and breadcrumbs into a food processor fitted with a standard blade. Chop 2 to 3 minutes or until finely mixed.

2. Mix juice-bread purée with salsa and cilantro.

3. Then return mixture to the food processor in 2-cup portions. Chop 2 to 3 minutes or until mixture is somewhat chunky.

4. Marinate for at least 1 hour before serving.

Appetizing Extras

You can actually make gazpacho with almonds, avocado, beets, and even strawberries or cherries.

Chickpea Dip

Similar to a hummus spread, this dip is great to serve with fresh, crusty bread, crackers, or crudités.

2 cups or 15 oz. can *chickpeas*, drained

3 piquillo peppers or small, roasted red peppers, seeds and ribs removed

4 cloves garlic, minced

¼ cup extra-virgin olive oil

2 TB. freshly squeezed lemon juice

1 TB. sherry wine vinegar

⅛ tsp. Spanish paprika

Yield: 2 cups
Prep Time: 5 minutes
Serving Size: About 3 tablespoons

1. Place chickpeas, peppers, garlic, olive oil, lemon juice, vinegar, and paprika into a food processor fitted with a standard chopping blade. Chop 2 to 3 minutes or until puréed.

2. Serve with crusty bread, crackers, or crudités.

Hablo Tapas

Chickpeas are legumes commonly found around the Mediterranean and are also known as garbanzo beans.

Variation: Easily turn this delicious dip into the more substantial hummus spread by simply adding ½ cup tahini or sesame paste.

5

Tortillas y Mas (Potato and Egg Dishes)

In This Chapter

◆ *Tortilla Español*

◆ *Ensalada rusa*

◆ Stuffed eggs

Perhaps the most quintessential of all cold tapas is *tortilla Español*. Unlike the Mexican, flat flour or corn tortilla, the Spanish tortilla is a thick egg and potato omelet.

Though Spanish tortillas are well-known, plenty of other egg and potato cold tapas are just as tasty, including my absolute favorite, *ensalada rusa* or Russian potato salad. Another quite tasty dish is *huevos rellenos* or stuffed eggs.

While it might seem a little odd not to include potato dishes in the vegetable chapter, potatoes often are served with eggs, most notably in the tortilla but also in most potato salads, too.

Ensalada Rusa with Marinated Tomatoes From Emilio's Restaurant, Hillside, IL

After leaving Spain, I searched and searched for the perfect *ensalada rusa* recipe, but every recipe and variation I tried didn't taste quite right … until I asked for this recipe from Emilio's Restaurant. The marinated tomatoes make the difference.

2 Roma tomatoes, seeded and chopped

1 TB. sherry wine vinegar

1 TB. extra-virgin olive oil

$\frac{1}{8}$ tsp. Kosher or sea salt

Freshly ground white pepper

2 large Idaho potatoes

1 large carrot

1 cup Spanish tuna fish, packed in oil

1 cup green peas

$\frac{1}{2}$ red bell pepper, diced

1 hard-boiled egg, chopped

$1\frac{1}{2}$ cups mayonnaise, homemade or Hellmann's

Yield: About 1 quart
Prep Time: 20 minutes
Chill Time: 1 hour
Cook Time: 20 to 30 minutes
Serving Size: About $\frac{1}{2}$ cup

1. Combine tomatoes, vinegar, olive oil, salt, and pepper, and marinate for at least 1 hour. Set aside.

2. Boil potatoes and carrot with skins on until soft but not mushy, about 20 minutes. Cool, remove skins, and dice vegetables.

3. Mix carrot, potatoes, tuna, peas, red pepper, and egg. Fold in mayonnaise. Season with salt and pepper to taste.

4. Top with marinated tomatoes and serve.

Appetizing Extras

Though I often make this recipe when I am serving tapas, this is also the perfect summer potato salad. Portion over mixed greens, and serve with a crusty baguette.

Light *Ensalada Rusa* with Marinated Tomatoes

I adore *ensalada rusa*, but it is one of the most fattening potato salads on the planet. In search of healthier fare, I developed this tapas which is still quite delicious.

2 Roma tomatoes, seeded and chopped

3 TB. sherry wine vinegar

$1/8$ tsp. Kosher or sea salt

Freshly ground white pepper

2 large Idaho potatoes

2 large carrots

$1/2$ large sweet potato

$1/2$ cup yellow or white onion, finely diced

1 cup tuna fish, packed in water

1 cup green peas

$1/2$ red bell pepper, diced

1 hard-boiled egg, chopped

$1/2$ cup low-fat yogurt

$1/2$ cup low-fat sour cream

1 TB. freshly squeezed lemon juice

1 tsp. lemon zest

1 tsp. Dijon mustard

Yield: About 1 quart
Prep Time: 20 minutes
Chill Time: 1 hour
Serving Size: About $1/2$ cup

1. Combine tomatoes, vinegar, salt, and pepper, and marinate for at least 1 hour. Set aside.

2. Boil potatoes, sweet potato, and carrots with skins on until soft but not mushy, about 20 minutes. Cool, remove skins, and dice vegetables.

3. Mix carrots, potatoes, onion, tuna, peas, red pepper, and egg.

4. Whisk together yogurt, sour cream, lemon juice, lemon zest, mustard. Season with salt and pepper, to taste.

5. Fold yogurt mixture into vegetable mixture, and serve topped with marinated tomatoes.

Tapas Tricks

Although low-fat yogurt and sour cream are lower in calories, you can use low-fat or no-fat mayonnaise, too.

Patatas con Alioli

This is another popular Spanish potato salad, which is quite garlicky.

4 Yukon gold potatoes

2 cups Alioli Sauce (recipe in Chapter 3)

$\frac{1}{2}$ tsp. sea salt

Freshly ground white pepper

2 TB. fresh chives, minced

1 hard-boiled egg, chopped (optional)

Yield: About 1 quart
Prep Time: 10 minutes
Cook Time: 20 minutes
Chill Time: 1 hour
Serving Size: About $\frac{1}{2}$ cup

1. Boil potatoes with skins on until soft but not mushy, about 20 minutes. Cool, remove skins, and dice potatoes.

2. In a bowl, mix together potatoes, Alioli Sauce, salt, and pepper.

3. Divide among serving plates, top with chives and/or egg. Serve with crusty bread.

Variation: For smaller, individual tapas, spoon potato salad on the leaves of endive lettuce or Asian soup spoons.

Tapas Tricks

You can use other potatoes like Idaho, but Yukon gold tend to have more flavor.

Tortilla Español

Also known as *tortilla de patatas* or potato tortilla, this is the classic Spanish tortilla. Just a few simple ingredients make this hearty tapas dish a delicious treat.

4 TB. extra-virgin olive oil

½ cup yellow or white onion, diced

1 large potato, boiled, peeled, and sliced

6 eggs, whisked together in a bowl

Salt and pepper

> **Yield: 1 large tortilla or four tapas servings**
>
> **Prep Time:** 15 minutes
>
> **Cook Time:** 10 to 15 minutes
>
> **Serving Size:** ¼ wedge

1. Heat skillet over medium-high heat for 1 to 2 minutes. Add 2 tablespoons olive oil and onion to the skillet. Sauté until well-cooked and onions are translucent, 2 to 5 minutes.

2. Add potato, eggs, salt, and pepper. Mix together to cook layers of egg using a spatula, but after mixing about 2 minutes, let bottom set up.

3. Scrape edge of mixture from the edge of the pan, pushing toward the middle but not slicing through. Push gently so a thick omelet comes together.

4. When all but the very top layer has cooked, remove the pan from heat. Using a spatula, loosen tortilla's edges. Then take a large plate, cover the pan, and flip the pan over. Use hot mitts so you don't burn your hands.

5. Add remaining 2 tablespoons olive oil to the pan and slide tortilla back into the pan. Cook 2 to 3 minutes until done with both sides slightly brown.

6. Flip tortilla onto a plate and cut into four, equal-size wedges. Serve hot or cold. Add a dollop of *Salsa Rosa* for color.

Appetizing Extras

The recipe Senora Ramona taught me called for using more oil and cooking the potatoes and onion together. If you wish to cook the potatoes and onion together, use at least ½ cup oil, and it takes at least 15 minutes for potatoes to cook.

Pepper, Tomato, and Ham Tortilla

The variations of Spanish tortilla are almost endless. This spicy, flavorful tortilla can even be served as a breakfast omelet.

3 TB. extra-virgin olive oil

6 eggs, whisked together in a bowl

3 slices Serrano ham, sliced into thin strips

2 piquillo peppers, thinly sliced or ¼ cup diced, red pepper

3 sun-dried tomatoes, thinly sliced, removed from oil

Salt and pepper

2 TB. hard Spanish cheese like Manchego or Iberico, grated

> **Yield: 1 large tortilla or four tapas servings**
>
> **Prep Time:** 10 minutes
>
> **Cook Time:** 10 to 15 minutes
>
> **Serving Size:** ¼ wedge

1. Heat a skillet over medium-high heat for 1 to 2 minutes. Add 2 tablespoons olive oil and heat for 1 minute. Add eggs, ham, peppers, tomatoes, salt, and pepper. Using a spatula, mix together to cook egg layers, but after about 2 minutes, let bottom set up.

2. Add cheese. Scrape the edge of the pan, pushing toward the middle, but not slicing through. Push gently so a thick omelet comes together.

3. When all but top layers have cooked, remove the pan from the heat. Using a spatula, loosen edges of tortilla. Then take a large plate, cover the pan, and flip it over. Use hot mitts so you don't burn your hands.

4. Add remaining 1 tablespoon olive oil to the pan and slide tortilla back into the pan. Cook 2 to 3 minutes until done. Both sides of omelet should be slightly brown.

5. Flip omelet onto a plate and cut into four, equal-size wedges. Serve hot or cold. Add a dollop of *Salsa Rosa* for color or a spoonful of Alioli Sauce for flavor.

> **Tapas Tricks**
>
> When serving, sprinkle Spanish paprika around the edge of the plate for a dramatic flair.

Shrimp and Asparagus Tortilla

A tortilla I enjoyed on the coast of Galicia in northwestern Spain inspired this variation.

3 TB. extra-virgin olive oil

6 eggs, whisked together in a bowl

½ cup cooked shrimp, diced

¼ cup cooked asparagus, diced

1 tsp. fresh dill, chopped

Salt and pepper

> **Yield: 1 large tortilla or four tapas servings**
>
> **Prep Time:** 5 minutes
>
> **Cook Time:** 10 to 15 minutes
>
> **Serving Size:** ¼ wedge

1. Heat a skillet over medium-high heat for 1 to 2 minutes. Add 2 table-spoons olive oil and heat for 1 minute. Add eggs, shrimp, asparagus, salt, and pepper. Mix together to cook egg layers using a spatula, but after about 2 minutes, let bottom set up.

2. Add dill. Scrape mixture from the edge of the pan, pushing toward the middle, but not slicing through. Push gently so a thick omelet comes together.

3. When all but top layers have cooked, remove the pan from the heat. Using a spatula, loosen edges of tortilla. Then take a large plate, cover the pan, and flip it over. Use hot mitts so you don't burn your hands.

4. Add remaining 1 tablespoon olive oil to the pan and slide tortilla back into the pan. Cook 2 to 3 minutes until done, with both sides slightly brown.

5. Flip omelet onto a plate and cut into four, equal-size wedges. Serve hot or cold. Add a dollop of *Salsa Rosa* for color or a spoonful of Alioli Sauce or Lemon *Mayonesa* for flavor.

Appetizing Extras

Shrimp tortilla or *tortilla de gambas* is one of the few dishes I enjoyed in Spain in which the shells and heads were removed from the shrimp before serving.

Huevos Rellenos

These are the best deviled eggs on the planet. *Huevos rellenos*, hands down, takes this simple dish to a new level. They are quite addictive.

6 eggs

¼ cup Spanish tuna or tuna packed in oil

¼ cup homemade mayonnaise or Lemon *Mayonesa*

4 pitted olives like kalamatas

¼ tsp. capers

2 tsp. sherry wine vinegar

1 tsp. Dijon mustard

Salt and pepper

Spanish paprika

Yield: 12 stuffed eggs
Prep Time: 15 minutes
Cook Time: 10 minutes
Cool Time: 10 minutes
Assemble: 5 minutes
Serving Size: 2 eggs

1. Put eggs in a pot and cover with 1 inch of water, and warm over high heat. When the water reaches a rolling boil, reduce heat to medium, and let boil for 10 minutes. Remove from hot water with a slotted spoon, and then let sit in cold water for an additional 10 minutes to cool down so that your fingers are not burned. Remove shells, slice in half, and reserve yolks.

2. Mix together yolks, tuna, mayonnaise, olives, capers, vinegar, mustard, salt, and pepper in a food processor fitted with a standard chopping blade. Chop or process for 1 to 2 minutes.

3. Put 1 rounded teaspoon filling in each egg half. Sprinkle with paprika and serve.

Variation: Instead of tuna, you can use smoked salmon for a stronger flavor. Use poached salmon or canned salmon. Leave out the pitted olives and sherry wine vinegar, and add one piquillo pepper. Or, try Serrano ham (use 4 slices) or any kind of ham that is finely chopped.

Tapas Tricks

You can use just about any extra bits of cooked veggies, meats, or seafood as an egg filling. This is a great tapas to make if you have other leftovers.

6

Cold Meat and Seafood Dishes

In This Chapter

- ◆ Spanish ham
- ◆ Salads
- ◆ Dips

Compared to the other recipe chapters, this one is short, but tasty. Though we frequently serve cold meat and seafood dishes as tapas, most often the meats or seafoods are just served as they are, on a plate or with some toasted bread.

Perhaps the most popular cold meat tapas dish is just Spanish ham, served with bread. Sometimes it is also plated with tomatoes or cheese, but typically, it is served just by itself. Spanish ham is quite a delight. You can use it in any of your own appetizer recipes that call for ham, and it is especially good for any sandwich-type appetizers. You can also serve cured Spanish chorizo or sausage, plain, with bread or just by itself.

Ham isn't the only cold meat you can use for your tapas. Chilled, cooked tenderloin can also be added to dishes, as can chilled, cooked chicken. Cold meats and chilled seafood lend themselves quite nicely to salads of mixed greens. Add chilled prawns or shrimp to chef and Cobb salads, and Spanish ham is great when paired with greens and extra-virgin olive oil.

Dips and pâtés are also great ways to enjoy meats and seafoods as a cold tapas.

Salad Accented with Iberico or Serrano Ham

Just about anything tastes better with a bit of dry-cured ham, and mixed greens are no exception.

½ cup extra-virgin olive oil

½ cup white or sherry wine vinegar

2 TB. shallots, finely diced

1 tsp. Dijon vinegar

Salt and freshly ground pepper

4 cups mixed greens

1 red pepper, thinly sliced

1 cup Mandarin oranges, drained

¼ cup grated hard cheese, like Manchego or Parmesan

8 slices of Iberico or Serrano ham, cut into thin, vertical strips

Yield: 4 servings
Prep Time: 15 minutes
Serving Size: 1 cup salad plus ham and vegetable portions

1. In a bowl, whisk together olive oil, vinegar, shallots, Dijon mustard, salt, and pepper. Set aside.

2. Place 1 cup mixed greens on four separate plates. Arrange peppers and oranges in a spiral pattern from the middle of each mound of greens. Sprinkle grated cheese over each salad. Then curl ham into little spirals around the edge of each plate. Drizzle with dressing and serve.

Tapas Tricks

If you can't get Serrano or Iberico ham, proscuitto is a good substitute.

Serrano Ham Wrapped Melon Pieces

This is a new twist on an old favorite, but instead of using the more common proscuitto, try Serrano ham or, if you're willing to pay a bit more, use the delectable Iberico ham.

8 slices Iberico or Serrano ham

8 large chunks cantaloupe

8 large chunks honeydew melon

¼ cup of extra-virgin olive oil

Salt and freshly ground pepper

Yield: 4 servings
Prep Time: 10 minutes
Serving Size: 4 melon pieces

1. Cut each piece of ham in half. Wrap one ham slice around each melon piece. Secure with a toothpick.

2. Place two cantaloupe slices and two honeydew slices on each plate. Drizzle with olive oil, season with salt and pepper, and serve.

 Tapas Tricks

Instead of melon, use peeled and segmented pieces of grapefruit or even watermelon. For an extra bit of eye candy, garnish with fresh mint leaves.

Tuna Stuffed Cherry Tomatoes

These bite-size tapas offer a punch of flavor and are pop-in-your-mouth favorites.

24 cherry tomatoes

1 (6 oz.) can tuna, packed in oil

4 TB. mayonnaise, homemade or Hellmann's

2 TB. grated hard cheese, like Parmesan or Manchego

2 TB. yellow or white onion, finely diced

2 TB. pitted olives, like kalamatas, finely diced

1 TB. capers (optional)

2 tsp. fresh lemon juice

1 tsp. Dijon mustard

1 tsp. Spanish paprika

Salt and pepper

Spanish paprika to garnish

Yield: 4 servings
Prep Time: 25 minutes
Refrigeration Time: 2 hours
Serving Size: 6 filled tomatoes

1. Slice tops off tomatoes. Using a small spoon, scoop out pulp and seeds. Sprinkle with salt and set aside.

2. In a large bowl, combine tuna, mayonnaise, cheese, onion, olives, capers (if using), lemon juice, mustard, paprika, salt, and pepper.

3. Using a spoon, fill tomatoes with about 1 to 2 teaspoons tuna mixture. Sprinkle paprika on top. Chill for 2 hours and serve.

 Tapas Tricks

> If the cherry tomatoes at your grocery store do not look good, use Roma tomatoes. But instead of 24, you'll need only 6 to 8 tomatoes. You also can sprinkle some fresh herbs like dill or thyme on top for variety.

Karen's Crab Dip with a Spanish Flair

Crab dip is more of an American hors d'oeuvre, but my bilingual sister Karen makes hers with a Castillian flair.

1 (6 oz.) can crab meat, water drained

8 oz. garlic and herb cream cheese

1/3 cup mayonnaise, homemade or Hellmann's

1/4 cup grated hard cheese, like Parmesan or Manchego

2 cloves garlic, minced

1 TB. Spanish paprika

1 TB. fresh chives, minced

Yield: 2 cups
Prep Time: 5 minutes
Serving Size: 2 to 4 tablespoons with crackers or chips

1. In a bowl, mix crab meat, cream cheese, mayonnaise, cheese, garlic, paprika, and chives until well blended.

2. Serve with crackers, toasted baguettes, or even crudités.

Tapas Tricks

Remember when your mom used to fill celery sticks with cream cheese or peanut butter? Update that classic childhood favorite simply by using this dip to fill celery sticks. (But don't top it with raisins … they don't go well with crab.)

Chicken Liver Pâté

Pâté is a quintessential Mediterranean appetizer, not just a French affair, and Spain serves up its share of this type of potted meat product. This pâté recipe is a variation of my stepmother-in-law Sarah Dowhower's appetizer.

20 oz. chicken livers, fat trimmed, cleaned, and cut into small pieces

1 yellow or white onion, thinly sliced

1 stick (8 oz.) unsalted butter

1 cup, plus 1 TB. Madeira port or sherry wine

1 TB. capers, preferably imported Spanish variety, drained and minced

1 (2 oz.) can salted anchovies, drained and minced

Salt and pepper

Yield: 2 cups

Prep Time: 15 minutes

Cook Time: 30 minutes

Chill Time: 1 hour

Serving Size: 2 to 4 tablespoons with crackers or chips

1. Over medium heat in a medium-size saucepan, sauté chicken livers and onion in butter for about 10 minutes. Add 1 cup wine and cook until evaporated.

2. Finely chop livers and onion. Mix with capers, anchovies, and remaining tablespoon wine.

3. Heat mixture until it is bubbly. Add salt and pepper. Serve hot, or chill in refrigerator for 1 hour. Serve on toasted baguettes or crackers.

 Tapas Tricks

Spread over toasted baguettes, topped with a sprig or two of fresh parsley, for canapés.

Honey Chorizo Spread

This was a tapas dish I was served at the El Foro Restaurant in Toledo, Spain.

2 links Spanish chorizo, uncooked but sliced into ½-inch pieces

⅓ cup honey

Yield: About ¾ cup

Prep Time: 5 minutes

Cook Time: 8 minutes

Chill Time: 1 hour

Serving Size: 1 to 2 tablespoons

1. In a medium-size saucepan, cook chorizo over high heat for about 6 to 8 minutes.

2. In a food processor fitted with a standard blade, chop chorizo and honey until chunky but well combined or about 5 minutes. Marinate for at least 1 hour. Serve with crackers or bread.

Appetizing Extras

After tasting this delightful dish, I asked for the recipe, but the chef explained to me that he didn't have a recipe—it was just chorizo and honey that he combined by taste.

Hot Tapas

This part is the heart of the cookbook—the hot, savory, and spicy dishes from Spain. Many of these dishes are the tapas people first think of when they go to a Spanish restaurant. This part includes hot recipes for meats and seafood, vegetables, potato and egg dishes, and even some international recipes for tapas, as well.

Chapter 7

Hot Vegetable Tapas

In This Chapter

◆ Stuffed vegetables

◆ Vegetable pastries

◆ Sautéed vegetables

◆ Garlic soup

Savory and sweet, hearty and filling, these vegetable tapas dishes can make a delicious meal all by themselves. Some of them, like *pisto manchego* and spinach, raisins, and pine nuts, you can serve as a base for meat.

Many of them, however, contain no eggs or milk, making them perfectly acceptable to your vegan friends. Plus, they are so savory and exotic, your meat-loving friends will also likely find them irresistible.

This chapter explores the art of making hot vegetable tapas. These dishes feature a variety of vegetables, including spinach, mushrooms, eggplant, asparagus, and artichokes. Some require little cooking or preparation, while others might take a bit more time.

Catalan Spinach with Garlic, Pine Nuts, and Raisins

This common dish in Cataluna is often served with fish, meat, and even eggs but tastes equally good by itself.

4 TB. extra-virgin olive oil

8 cups fresh baby spinach leaves

4 cloves garlic, minced

1 cup diced apple

¼ cup pine nuts

¼ cup raisins, preferably golden

Salt and pepper

Yield: 2 cups
Cook Time: 10 minutes
Serving Size: ½ cup

1. Heat a skillet over medium-high heat for 1 to 2 minutes. Add olive oil and heat for 1 minute. Add spinach and garlic, and cook about 2 minutes or until spinach begins to wilt.

2. Add apple, pine nuts, and raisins, and sauté for 2 to 3 minutes. Remove from heat and serve.

 Tapas Tricks

While you can serve this tapas dish by itself, it also makes a great base for pork tenderloin and chicken tapas dishes or a side dish for other Mediterranean recipes.

Vegetarian Spinach and Caramelized Onion *Empanadas*

Just about any cooked vegetable works—potatoes, beans, chickpeas—in *empanadas*, but to me, spinach and caramelized onion *empanadas* are the best.

2 TB. extra-virgin olive oil

1/2 cup yellow or white onion, diced

2 cloves of garlic, minced

2 cups fresh spinach

1/4 cup pine nuts

1/4 cup raisins

3 TB. grated hard cheese like Manchego or Iberico

2 TB. crème fraîche or cream cheese

1 TB. sherry wine

Salt and pepper

2 sheets prepared puff pastry dough, thawed

1 egg, beaten and set aside for egg wash

Alioli Sauce, *Salsa Rosa*, or Lemon *Mayonesa* (recipes in Chapter 3)

Yield: 18 *empanadas*
Prep Time: 15 minutes
Cook Time: 20 minutes
Serving Size: 2 to 3 *empanadas*

1. Preheat oven to 350°F.

2. Heat a skillet over medium-high heat for 1 minute. Add oil and heat for 1 to 2 minutes. Add onion and sauté until caramelized. Add garlic and spinach; sauté for 1 minute. Remove from heat.

3. Put onion, garlic, spinach, pine nuts, raisins, cheese, crème fraîche, and sherry into a food processor fitted with a standard chopping blade. Chop until fine, or process about 2 minutes. Season with salt and pepper, to taste.

4. In puff pastry, cut circles 4-inch in diameter. Put 1 rounded teaspoon in the middle of each circle. Fold circle over, pinching ends together and crimping with fingers to look pretty. Brush with egg wash.

5. Bake in the oven for 20 minutes. Serve with Alioli Sauce, *Salsa Rosa*, or Lemon *Mayonesa*.

Appetizing Extras

The Catalan dish of spinach, pine nuts, raisins, and garlic inspired the filling of this *empanada*.

Variations: Instead of spinach, try cooked asparagus and goat cheese (just eliminate the raisins and pine nuts). Also try puréed chickpeas or other legumes.

Stewed Spinach and Chickpeas

This hearty dish can be served by itself or topped with meat, seafood, or even poached eggs.

1 TB. extra-virgin olive oil

1 cup yellow or white onion, diced

8 cloves garlic, minced

4 cups fresh baby spinach leaves

2 (15 oz.) cans chickpeas, drained

1 cup chicken or vegetable broth

4 TB. tomato sauce

¼ tsp. Spanish paprika

¼ tsp. nutmeg

¼ tsp. cinnamon

¼ tsp. sea salt

½ cup pine nuts

Yield: 6 cups
Prep Time: 5 minutes
Cook Time: 15 minutes
Serving Size: 1 cup

1. Heat a large skillet over medium-high heat for 1 minute. Add oil and heat for 1 to 2 minutes. Add onion and sauté until caramelized, about 5 minutes.

2. Add garlic and spinach. Sauté until spinach wilts, about 1 minute. Remove the spinach and then continue with recipe.

3. Add chickpeas, broth, tomato sauce, paprika, nutmeg, cinnamon, salt, and pine nuts. Reduce heat to medium or medium-low, and simmer for at least 15 minutes. Add spinach.

4. Remove from heat, and serve alone or top it with meat, seafood, or eggs.

 Appetizing Extras

Kate, the blogger at veggiefriendly.com.au became a tapas convert after eating some tasty spinach tapas; prior to dining at the Cantina Bar and Grill in Sydney, she had always believed that Spanish food was not conducive to vegetarians.

Spinach and Caramelized Onion Flan

Though flan is typically a sweet dessert, it can also be a savory vegetable tapas.

1 TB. extra-virgin olive oil

1 cup yellow or white onion, diced

2 cups fresh baby spinach leaves

1 cup heavy cream

4 eggs, beaten

¼ cup Manchego, grated

¼ tsp. grated nutmeg

⅛ tsp. sea salt

Freshly ground white pepper

Butter for lining ramekins or custard dishes

Yield: 4 servings

Prep Time: 10 minutes

Cook Time: 50 minutes to 1 hour

Serving Size: ½ cup

1. Heat a large skillet over medium-high heat for 1 minute. Add oil and heat for 1 to 2 minutes. Add onion and sauté until caramelized or about 5 minutes.

2. Add spinach. Sauté until spinach wilts about 1 minute.

3. Preheat oven to 350°F.

4. In a food processor fitted with a standard blade, add onion, spinach, cream, eggs, cheese, nutmeg, salt, and pepper. Chop for 2 minutes or until everything is smoothly blended.

5. Butter 4 ramekins or custard dishes. Line with pieces of waxed paper, cut to fit the bottom of the dishes. Butter top of waxed paper, and divide mixture evenly among dishes.

6. Place ramekins into a *bain marie* or cake dish. Fill the dish carefully with water until water is halfway up the ramekins. Then bake custards for 50 minutes to 1 hour or until a toothpick inserted comes out clean.

7. Remove from the oven, and cool for 5 minutes. Use a knife to loosen flans from the dish, and flip dishes onto serving plates. Remove waxed paper and serve.

Hablo Tapas

A **bain marie** is simply a French term for water bath. There are special bain marie dishes for cooking custards, but a cake pan will also do just fine.

Variation: Instead of spinach, use mushrooms, artichokes, or asparagus.

Stuffed Mushrooms

Sherry wine gives this tapas dish its decidedly Spanish flavor.

2 TB. extra-virgin olive oil

1 cup diced yellow or white onion

3 cloves garlic, minced

3 slices bacon, cooked and crumbed

½ cup panko breadcrumbs

2 TB. sherry wine

Salt and pepper

16 oz. mushrooms, stems removed

Yield: About 50 individual mushrooms
Prep Time: 10 minutes
Cook Time: 20 minutes
Serving Size: 5 mushrooms

1. Heat a skillet over medium-high heat for 1 to 2 minutes. Add olive oil, and heat 1 to 2 minutes. Add onion and cook until caramelized.

2. Add garlic, cook 1 to 2 minutes, and remove from heat.

3. In a separate bowl, mix together onion, garlic, bacon, breadcrumbs, wine, salt, and pepper. Put one rounded teaspoon mixture into each mushroom cap.

4. Preheat broiler on high. Cook mushrooms for 10 to 15 minutes.

 Tapas Tricks

If you don't want to broil these mushrooms, you can bake them at 350°F for 25 to 30 minutes.

Garlic-Sherry Mushrooms

Serve this simple but delicious dish in individual ramekins or in a giant bowl for your guests to sample.

4 TB. extra-virgin olive oil

8 oz. mushrooms, sliced in half

4 TB. diced yellow or white onion

4 cloves garlic, minced

4 TB. sherry wine

Juice from ½ lemon

⅛ tsp. oregano

⅛ tsp. Spanish paprika

⅛ tsp. salt

Freshly ground pepper

Yield: About 2 cups mushrooms
Prep Time: 5 minutes
Cook Time: 10 minutes
Serving Size: ½ cup

1. Heat a skillet over medium-high heat for 1 to 2 minutes. Add olive oil and heat for 1 minute. Add mushrooms, onion, and garlic, sautéing until vegetables are nearly cooked.

2. Add wine, lemon juice, oregano, paprika, salt, and pepper to vegetables. Cook 1 to 2 more minutes. Remove from heat and serve.

Variation: For canapés, simply spoon about a tablespoon over toasted bread points.

 Tapas Tricks

Though regular, white mushrooms work well, you can also use portobellas, shiitakes, and other types of mushrooms as well. Portobellos and shiitakes add a deeper flavor.

Warm Avocado and Tuna Dip

At a Spanish restaurant, I tried a similar dip made with cod. Using canned tuna is easier—but just as tasty.

4 TB. extra-virgin olive oil

½ cup yellow or white onions, diced

3 garlic cloves

3 oz. Spanish tuna, packed in oil

2 avocados, cut in half, pits removed

¼ tsp. Spanish paprika

Salt and pepper

Yield: 1 cup dip
Prep Time: 5 minutes
Cook Time: 10 minutes
Serving Size: ¼ cup

1. Heat a medium-size pot over medium-high heat for 1 to 2 minutes. Add 2 tablespoons olive oil, and heat for 1 minute. Add onions and garlic, sauté until caramelized, about 5 minutes.

2. Reduce heat to low, add tuna, and squeeze avocados into pot. Sauté for 2 to 5 minutes. Season with paprika, salt, and pepper.

3. Remove from heat. Use either a handheld blender, a blender, or a food processor to purée.

4. Serve with crackers or toasted baguette slices.

 Tapas Tricks

> Sort of like a Spanish guacamole, you can easily serve this dish as bite-size appetizers by spreading it on toasted baguette slices or crackers. Top with some minced parsley for garnish.

Asparagus and Artichoke Heart Gratin

This hearty, warm tapas dish uses homemade Alioli Sauce to give it a distinctive, savory flavor.

20 asparagus spears, ends chopped off

8 oz. marinated artichoke hearts

1 cup Alioli Sauce (recipe in Chapter 3)

¼ Manchego or Parmesan cheese, grated

2 TB. breadcrumbs

Yield: 4 servings
Prep Time: 5 minutes
Cook Time: 30 minutes
Serving Size: 4 to 5 spears, plus 2 artichoke hearts

1. In a medium-size pot, bring water to a boil. Drop asparagus into water and cook for 1 minute. Remove from heat, and immediately drain in cold water.

2. In a casserole dish, layer asparagus and artichokes with Alioli Sauce. Top with cheese and breadcrumbs.

3. Bake for 30 minutes. Serve immediately.

Variation: For some extra zip, use a crumbled blue cheese like Cabrales or Gorgonzola instead of Manchego or Parmesan. That takes this delicious gratin to a new height.

Vegetable Fritters

Known as *fritos*, vegetable fritters are Spain's answer to tempura ... and they are just as tasty. But instead of being served with tempura sauce or wasabi paste, serve them with Alioli or *Salsa Rosa*.

1 cup white flour

1 cup milk

2 eggs

2 cloves garlic, minced

¼ tsp. baking soda

¼ tsp. sea salt

⅛ tsp. Spanish paprika

4 cups olive oil

6 cups assorted vegetables like cauliflower, mushrooms, broccoli, or green beans

Alioli Sauce or *Salsa Rosa* (recipes in Chapter 3)

Yield: 6 cups
Prep Time: 10 minutes
Cook Time: 30 minutes
Serving Size: About ½ cup

1. Whisk together flour, milk, eggs, garlic, baking soda, salt, and paprika to make batter.

2. In a large pot, heat olive oil over medium-high heat. This will take at least 5 minutes as you want the oil to be almost sizzling.

3. Dip vegetables in batter, and drop carefully into hot oil. Do not add more than 10 vegetable pieces at a time; don't crowd the pan. Mushrooms will float to the top. Turn vegetables occasionally—every 2 minutes or so. Cook vegetables until golden brown.

4. As vegetables cook, remove them with a slotted spoon, drain on a paper towel, and continue to add new vegetables dipped in batter to oil. It will take about 30 minutes to cook all the vegetables.

5. Serve with Alioli Sauce or *Salsa Rosa*.

Hot 'n' Spicy

Cooking with oil can be a dangerous endeavor. Use a glass lid to shield yourself as you drop the vegetables into the hot oil. Wooden tongs, wooden spoons, and even wooden chop sticks are good for turning the vegetables in the oil because any metal utensils will heat up quickly and burn your fingers. When adding something to hot oil, put it in the pan in a motion that is away from your body.

Stuffed Eggplant

This very pretty salad can be dressed with the Orange-Sherry Vinaigrette or the Simple Sherry Vinaigrette (recipes in Chapter 4).

2 eggplants, cut in half

16 oz. tomato sauce

2 cups breadcrumbs

$1/2$ tsp. Spanish paprika

4 cloves garlic, minced

$1/2$ tsp. sea salt

$1/2$ cup grated Manchego cheese

$1/4$ cup extra-virgin olive oil

Yield: 4 servings
Prep Time: 10 minutes
Bake Time: 30 minutes
Serving Size: $1/2$ eggplant

1. Use a melon baller to scoop out middle of eggplant halves.

2. Preheat oven to 350°F.

Appetizing Extras

Eggplant originally hailed from India before it spread to Spain and other parts of the globe.

3. In a bowl, mix together tomato sauce, breadcrumbs, paprika, garlic, and salt. Divide breadcrumb mixture, and spoon into halves of eggplant. Top with cheese.

4. Drizzle olive oil on eggplant, especially edges. Bake for 30 minutes. Serve immediately.

Variation: For variety, mix in diced, cooked bacon or diced Serrano ham—use about $1/4$ cup.

Garlic Soup

Though gazpacho is famous, this common Spanish soup isn't well-known outside of the Iberian peninsula. It's similar to a French onion soup, except it's made with garlic instead of onions and not typically topped with cheese.

4 TB. extra-virgin olive oil

6 cloves garlic, sliced

2 cups torn, toasted baguette pieces

3 TB. sherry wine

1 tsp. Spanish paprika

6 cups chicken broth

4 eggs

Grated Manchego or Parmesan cheese

> **Yield: 4 servings**
> **Prep Time:** 5 minutes
> **Cook Time:** 15 minutes
> **Serving Size:** 1 cup

1. In a medium-size pot, heat olive oil over medium-high heat for 2 minutes. Add garlic and sauté for 2 minutes.

2. Add baguette pieces, wine, paprika, and broth. Reduce heat to medium, and simmer for 15 minutes.

3. Just before serving, crack eggs directly into soup. Poach for 3 to 5 minutes, until solid, but still runny if you cut into them.

4. Divide soup evenly among four bowls, including one egg per bowl. Sprinkle with paprika, or top with grated Manchego or Parmesan cheese.

Appetizing Extras

Whenever I make this dish, I think of my Spanish friend, Maria Jose, or *Ajo* (MariA Jose) to her friends. *Ajo*, in Spanish, means garlic.

Pisto Manchego

This dish is Spain's answer to ratatouille (a classic French dish of stewed vegetables). A hearty, vegetable dish, it can be served plain or as an accompaniment to meat or tortillas.

2 TB. extra-virgin olive oil

1 cup yellow or white onion, diced

1 red or green pepper, cored, seeded, and sliced

3 small zucchinis, sliced

4 tomatoes, seeded and roughly chopped

6 cloves garlic, minced

2 TB. red wine

1 tsp. dried oregano

½ tsp. Spanish paprika

¼ tsp. sea salt

Freshly ground pepper

¼ cup parsley or cilantro, finely chopped

Yield: About 4 cups
Prep Time: 10 minutes
Cook Time: 20 to 30 minutes
Serving Size: ½ cup

1. Heat a skillet over medium-high heat for 1 minute. Add olive oil and heat 1 minute. Add onion, pepper, zucchini, tomatoes, and garlic, and sauté for 5 minutes.

2. Add wine, oregano, paprika, salt, and pepper. Reduce heat and simmer for 20 to 30 minutes. Add parsley or cilantro for last 5 minutes of cooking.

Appetizing Extras _____

Though Manchego is in the name of this dish, it doesn't refer to the cheese. Instead, it means "of the region of La Mancha."

Marinated Vegetable Skewers

This tapas is an ideal dish for summer and can be an accompaniment to even hamburgers or grilled meats.

1 pint cherry tomatoes

8 oz. mushrooms

1 yellow squash, sliced

¼ cup extra-virgin olive oil

¼ cup sherry wine vinegar

2 cloves garlic, minced

¼ tsp. Spanish paprika

½ tsp. sea salt

Freshly ground pepper

Extra olive oil

Yield: About 3 cups
Prep Time: 10 minutes
Marinate Time: 30 minutes
Cook Time: 5 minutes
Serving Size: ½ cup or ½ skewer of vegetables

1. Using long wooden skewers, put vegetables on the skewers alternating tomato, mushroom, and squash.

2. In a bowl, whisk together olive oil, vinegar, garlic, paprika, salt, and pepper for marinade.

3. Place skewers in a large plastic bag with marinade. Shake to coat, and then refrigerate for at least 30 minutes.

4. Heat grill (if using electric, set to high setting). Place skewers on grill. Brush with extra olive oil. Grill for 2 to 4 minutes; then turn using tongs.

5. Serve either on skewers, or remove from skewers for serving.

Tapas Tricks

When making grilling marinades, always start with a base of oil, adding vinegar and wine, and then spices. For an Italian flavored marinade, use basil and oregano instead of paprika.

Artichokes with Cheese

This was a tapas dish served at the Restaurant Divino in Segovia, Spain.

¼ lb. Manchego, grated

12 artichoke bottoms or 2 (14 oz.) cans

Spanish paprika

Yield: 12 artichokes
Prep Time: 5 minutes
Cook Time: 5minutes
Serving Size: 2 artichokes

1. Preheat broiler to high. If the bottoms wobble when placed on cookie sheet, cut a sliver off of the bottom so that they stand.

2. Place bottoms on cookie sheet. Top with 1 to 2 tsp. of grated cheese and sprinkle with paprika. Broil for 5 minutes.

 Tapas Tricks

Artichoke bottoms are, well, the bottoms of artichokes, and they look like little cups. You can use artichoke hearts as a substitution, but if you use them, place them in a dish, then top with cheese, as you cannot as easily create individual portions with regular hearts.

Chapter 8

Hot Potato and Egg Tapas

In This Chapter

- ◆ *Patatas bravas*
- ◆ Spanish scrambled eggs
- ◆ Poached Andalusian eggs

Spicy and hearty, these hot potato and egg dishes are unlike most potato dishes around. Some are baked; some are fried; but all are packed with flavor.

While many cold potato and egg tapas dishes combine these two ingredients, most hot potato or egg dishes do not use both ingredients in a single dish. One commonality to many of these tapas is that they are flavored with Spanish paprika, and the heat from the paprika takes center stage.

Patatas bravas, a favorite from Catalonia, is one of the most popular tapas dishes around. Other dishes highlighted in this chapter include *revueltos* or Spanish scrambled eggs, and smoky, smashed potatoes with bacon and chorizo.

Patatas Bravas

Literally translated as "fierce potatoes," this tapas dish offers bold, spicy flavors. It's like fries with spicy ketchup or barbecue sauce.

1 TB. plus 1 cup extra-virgin olive oil

3 TB. red or yellow onion, finely diced

4 cloves garlic, minced

½ cup diced onion

8 oz. tomato sauce

2 tsp. white vinegar

1 tsp. Spanish paprika

1 tsp. sugar

½ tsp. dried oregano

¼ tsp. cayenne

⅛ tsp. cinnamon

2 large Idaho potatoes, peeled, sliced into fries, about ¼-inch thick

> **Yield: About 30 individual fries**
>
> **Prep Time:** 15 minutes
>
> **Cook Time:** 30 minutes
>
> **Serving Size:** 5 fries plus 1 or 2 tablespoons sauce

1. Heat a large skillet over medium-high heat for 1 minute. Add 1 tablespoon olive oil; heat for 1 minute; then add onion and garlic. Sauté 1 to 2 minutes.

2. Add tomato sauce, vinegar, paprika, sugar, oregano, cayenne, and cinnamon. Simmer about 5 minutes; remove from heat and set aside.

3. Heat 1 cup olive oil in a large pot over medium-high heat until it is sizzling.

4. In small batches, add fries to oil. Cook until browned on all sides, about 5 to 10 minutes. Don't crowd oil with too many fries. Use a glass lid to shield you from sizzling oil when adding, turning, or removing fries, but don't leave the lid on the pot.

5. Remove fries with slotted spoon, drain on paper towels, and serve with brava sauce on top or along side for dipping.

Tapas Tricks

Patatas bravas is often served with Alioli Sauce as well, with the garlic mayonnaise countering the spicy, hot sauce.

≈⌐⁓

Stuffed Potatoes with Caramelized Onions and Goat Cheese

This beats twice-baked potatoes any day ... plus, it's a perfect, easy-to-serve appetizer.

10 medium red potatoes

2 tsp. extra-virgin olive oil

1/2 cup diced onion

4 ounces crème fraîche or cream cheese

2 TB. fresh goat cheese

Salt and pepper

Spanish paprika

Yield: 10 stuffed potatoes
Prep Time: 15 minutes
Cook Time: 20 to 30 minutes
Serving Size: 2 potatoes

1. Preheat oven to 350°F.

2. Using a melon baller, scoop out large hole in each potato. Discard raw potato centers.

3. Heat a skillet over medium-high heat for 1 to 2 minutes. Add oil and heat for 1 minute. Add onions and sauté until caramelized, about 5 minutes. Let cool.

4. Place onions, crème fraîche, cheese, salt, and pepper into a food processor with a standard chopping blade. Process until smooth—about 1 minute.

5. Fill empty potatoes with 1 to 2 tablespoons cream mixture. Sprinkle with paprika, and bake for 20 to 30 minutes.

Variation: Substitute any kind of cheese for the goat cheese, including: blue, Parmesan, and Swiss.

Tapas Tricks _____

If you do not have a melon baller, you can use a small ice-cream scooper or a knife and a spoon.

Gratin Potatoes

Though packed with a punch of flavor, the focus of this dish is on garlic, not paprika.

4 cups *Patatas con Alioli* (recipe in Chapter 5)

½ cup grated Manchego or Parmesan cheese

½ tsp. sea salt

Freshly ground white pepper

Yield: 4 cups
Cook Time: 20 minutes
Serving Size: ½ cup

1. Preheat oven to 350°F.

2. Layer potatoes and alioli in a casserole dish. Sprinkle with cheese, salt, and pepper. Bake for 30 minutes. It will be slightly browned on top.

Tapas Tricks _____

For a more visual appeal, cook in individual ramekins or custard dishes.

Spanish Scrambled Eggs or *Revueltas* with Chorizo and Bacon

Spanish scrambled eggs are not cooked as hard as American scrambled eggs—they are soft and creamy, and as soon as they are cooked, they are served on the plate.

6 eggs, beaten

1 TB. heavy cream

3 slices of bacon

3 TB. yellow or white onion, finely diced

2 cloves garlic, minced

¼ cup sliced chorizo

1 TB. tomato sauce

1 tsp. paprika

1 to 2 TB. grated Manchego cheese (optional)

Yield: 4 servings
Prep Time: 10 minutes
Cook Time: 5 minutes
Serving Size: About 1½ eggs or ¼ egg mixture in the pan

1. Beat eggs and cream together. Set aside.

2. Heat a skillet over medium-high heat for 1 minute. Add bacon and cook until crisp. Drain on paper towels. Crumble.

3. In bacon grease over medium-high heat, cook onion, garlic, and chorizo. Add tomato sauce and paprika; then add egg-cream mixture.

4. Reduce heat to medium or medium-low, stirring to scramble. Remove from heat when eggs are still creamy and runny. Top with cheese and serve.

Appetizing Extras

Revueltas are also often known as *revolitas*, with the *lita* ending signifying a diminutive or translating as "little scrambles."

Spanish Scrambled Eggs or *Revueltas* with Asparagus and Shrimp

This version of *revueltas* is a bit healthier as it uses the more traditional olive oil instead of bacon grease.

6 eggs, beaten

1 TB. heavy cream

1 TB. extra-virgin olive oil

3 TB. yellow or white onion, finely diced

2 cloves garlic, minced

4 pickled white asparagus spears, diced

6 cooked shrimp, tails removed, diced

1 to 2 TB. fresh chèvre (optional)

> **Yield: 4 servings**
>
> **Prep Time:** 10 minutes
>
> **Cook Time:** 5 minutes
>
> **Serving Size:** About 1½ eggs or ¼ egg mixture in the pan

1. Beat eggs and cream together. Set aside.

2. Heat a skillet over medium-high heat for 1 minute. Add olive oil and heat for 1 minute. Add onion and garlic and sauté until translucent, about 2 to 3 minutes.

3. Add asparagus and shrimp and cook for 1 minute. Add egg-cream mixture.

4. Reduce heat to medium or medium-low, stirring to scramble. Remove from heat when eggs are still creamy and runny. Top with cheese (if using) and serve.

 Tapas Tricks _____

A tablespoon or two of fresh, chopped chives adds a little color and flavor to this dish. In Spain, *revueltas* are frequently topped with a drizzle of olive oil before serving.

Variation: For a vegetarian version, use ½ cup halved, pickled mushrooms and 3 sliced piquillo peppers instead of shrimp and asparagus.

Andalusian Poached Eggs

This is one of the spiciest egg dishes I have ever enjoyed. It is hearty and can be served at breakfast, lunch, or dinner.

2 TB. extra-virgin olive oil

4 TB. yellow or white onion, diced

4 cloves garlic, minced

6 piquillo peppers, julienned

1/2 cup chopped chorizo

2 cups fresh, mild salsa

1 TB. Spanish paprika

1/2 tsp. sea salt

8 eggs

1/2 cup grated Manchego cheese

Yield: 4 servings
Prep Time: 5 minutes
Cook Time: 10 minutes
Serving Size: 1 ramekin

1. Preheat oven to 400°F. Heat a large skillet over medium-high heat for 1 minute. Add oil and heat for 1 to 2 minutes. Add onion, sautéing until caramelized or about 5 minutes.

2. Add garlic, peppers, and chorizo. Sauté for 2 to 3 minutes. Then add salsa, paprika, and salt, and cook for another 3 to 5 minutes.

3. Divide mixture evenly among four ramekins, and crack 2 eggs onto each. Sprinkle with cheese, and bake for 10 minutes.

4. Serve immediately.

Tapas Tricks

Instead of chorizo, use three or four slices of cooked bacon or Serrano ham.

Fingerling Potatoes Wrapped in Serrano Ham

These little fried potatoes are good finger foods for parties. Fingerling potatoes are small, miniature potatoes that are great for using in appetizers.

1½ cup fingerling potatoes

4 slices Serrano ham, cut into narrow strips

1 cup extra-virgin olive oil

Alioli Sauce for dipping (recipe in Chapter 3)

Yield: 18 to 20 potatoes

Prep Time: 10 minutes

Cook Time: 30 minutes

Serving Size: 4 or 5 potatoes

1. Wrap slices of Serrano ham around potatoes and secure with a wooden toothpick.

2. Heat olive oil in a large pot over medium-high heat for at least 5 minutes until oil is almost bubbling. When oil is heated, add potatoes, one small batch at a time.

3. Use wooden spoons or tongs to turn potatoes so they brown evenly on all sides. Cook 5 to 10 minutes or until a nice, golden brown color.

4. Remove potatoes from heat using a slotted spoon, drain on paper towels, and serve with Alioli Sauce for dipping.

Hot 'n' Spicy

Anytime you cook with a ½ cup or more oil, be very careful because hot oil sometimes sizzles and snaps. Use a glass lid to protect your face when you drop, turn, or remove potatoes from the pot.

Smoky, Smashed Potatoes

Paprika, chorizo, and Serrano ham make this a hearty and spicy dish. It is a great tapas to pair with meat dishes, but it is more than a meal in itself.

4 Yukon gold potatoes, cut into pieces, skins removed

6 cloves garlic

1 TB. extra-virgin olive oil

½ cup yellow or white onion, diced

3 slices Serrano ham

¼ cup Spanish chorizo

2 TB. tomato sauce

¼ tsp. Spanish paprika

¼ cup milk

4 TB. unsalted butter

½ tsp. salt

Freshly ground white pepper

Yield: About 4 cups
Prep Time: 10 minutes
Cook Time: 20 minutes
Serving Size: ½ cup

1. In a large pot of water over medium-high heat, bring potatoes and garlic to a boil and cook until soft, at least 10 minutes.

2. Heat a skillet over medium-high heat for 1 minute. Add olive oil and heat for 1 to 2 minutes. Add onions and sauté until caramelized, about 5 minutes. Remove from heat.

3. Drain potatoes and garlic. Return to the pot, and mash with ham, onion, chorizo, tomato sauce, paprika, milk, butter, salt, and pepper until most lumps are removed.

4. Serve immediately.

Appetizing Extras

In Spain, most versions of this dish use extra-virgin olive oil instead of butter, but I just simply think that mashed potatoes taste better with butter.

Chapter 9

Hot Meat and Seafood Dishes

In This Chapter

- *Empanadas*
- Paella balls
- Garlic shrimp and beef skewers

Hot meat and seafood dishes are some of the most popular tapas dishes in tapas restaurants. They are sort of the "entrée" of tapas, and in fact, if you simply increase the serving size, you can serve some of these dishes as entrées as well.

These dishes come in great variety. Savory and sometimes sweet or spicy, they can feature shrimp or tuna, beef or chicken, and, of course, ham and pork. Some of these dishes are fried, others are baked, and some are cooked on the stove or in the oven.

Arroz con Pollo or Spanish Chicken and Rice

This is a very common, basic chicken dish in Spain, but it tastes so good.

½ cup white flour

1 tsp. Spanish paprika

1 tsp. dried oregano

Salt and pepper

6 boneless, skinless chicken breasts, legs, or thighs

4 TB. extra-virgin olive oil

¼ tsp. or pinch saffron (optional)

5 cups chicken stock or chicken broth

1 cup yellow or white onion, finely diced

3 cloves garlic, finely minced

8 oz. sliced mushrooms

1 cup chopped tomatoes

2 cups short-grained white rice, like Arborio

Yield: 6 servings
Prep Time: 30 minutes
Cook Time: 30 minutes
Serving Size: 1 chicken breast and ⅓ cup rice

1. In a large bowl, mix together flour, paprika, oregano, salt, and pepper. Dredge chicken in flour mixture.

2. Heat nonstick skillet over medium-high heat for 1 minute. Add 2 tablespoons olive oil, and heat for another minute. Add chicken and sauté until golden or about 3 minutes per side. Set aside on platter.

3. If using saffron, dissolve it in chicken broth, and set aside.

4. Heat a large pot over medium-high heat for 1 minute. Add remaining olive oil, and heat for another minute. Add onion, garlic, and mushrooms, and sauté for about 4 minutes or until vegetables are cooked. Add tomatoes and cook for another 2 minutes.

5. Add rice, broth, and chicken, bring to a boil, then cover and simmer until rice is cooked and most of the liquid is absorbed, about 25 to 30 minutes.

Appetizing Extras _____

Arroz con pollo is one of those Spanish dishes that has spread through Central and South America. It is so popular that there is even a Latin restaurant of the same name in Orlando, Florida.

Chicken Breasts with Rosemary and Cherries

Though cherries aren't really a popular fruit in Spain, I enjoyed a similar dish once at a Spanish restaurant in the United States. They are really popular in northern Spain and also the Basque Country.

6 boneless, skinless chicken breasts

Salt and pepper

$\frac{1}{2}$ cup flour

1 tsp. Spanish paprika

5 TB. extra-virgin olive oil

$\frac{1}{2}$ cup yellow or white onion, finely diced

3 cloves garlic, finely minced

1 tsp. Dijon mustard

1 tsp. honey

$\frac{1}{2}$ tsp. sea salt

$\frac{1}{2}$ cup white or sherry wine

1 cup canned tart cherries, drained, $\frac{1}{4}$ cup cherry juice reserved

2 tsp. cornstarch

1 TB. loosely packed rosemary, finely minced after measuring

Yield: 6 servings
Prep Time: 1 hour
Cook Time: 30 minutes; 15 minutes for chicken, 15 minutes for cherry sauce
Serving Size: 1 chicken breast plus $\frac{1}{3}$ cup cooked rice

1. Trim fat off chicken; then salt and pepper, dredge in flour, sprinkle with paprika, and set aside.

2. Heat 3 tablespoons olive oil over medium-high heat in a skillet. Add onions and garlic, and sauté for 2 minutes. Whisk in mustard, honey, sea salt, wine, and cherries, and cook 2 minutes.

3. Mix remaining cherry juice with cornstarch, and add to mixture. Cook until thickened to salsa consistency. Add rosemary and remove from heat.

4. Heat skillet over medium-high heat for 1 minute. Add remaining 2 tablespoons olive oil and heat another minute. Add chicken and cook until browned and no longer pink inside, about 10 to 15 minutes.

5. When chicken is cooked, warm up sauce. Serve chicken on bed of rice, spoon cherry sauce over top, and garnish with extra rosemary.

Appetizing Extras

Rosemary, an herb that hails from the Mediterranean, has the official name of *rosemarinus officinalis*, which means dew of the sea. In Spanish, the herb is called *romero*. But any way you call it, rosemary adds an aromatic touch to your dishes.

Baked Tuna *Empanadas*

You can bake or fry *empanadas*, but it is easier to bake them. Though I have made *empanada* dough, using puff pastry dough makes the process very simple.

3 oz. Spanish tuna, packed in oil

½ cup pitted olives, like kalamatas

½ cup raisins

1 hard-boiled egg

3 TB. tomato sauce

1 TB. sherry wine

½ tsp. oregano

¼ tsp. Spanish paprika

Salt and pepper

2 sheets prepared puff pastry dough, thawed

1 egg, beaten and set aside

Yield: 18 *empanadas*

Prep Time: 15 minutes

Cook Time: 20 minutes

Serving Size: 2 to 3 *empanadas*

1. Preheat oven to 350°F. Put tuna, olives, raisins, egg, tomato sauce, wine, oregano, paprika, salt, and pepper into a food processor. Chop until fine, or process for about 2 minutes.

2. Cut circles 4 inches in diameter in puff pastry. Put 1 rounded tea-spoon tuna mixture in the middle of each circle. Fold circle over, pinching ends together and crimping with fingers to look pretty. Brush with egg.

3. Bake in oven for 20 minutes. Serve with Alioli Sauce, *Salsa Rosa*, or Lemon *Mayonesa*.

Tapas Tricks

If your grocery store doesn't sell puff pastry dough in the frozen food aisle, crescent roll dough, pressed flat with a rolling pin, is a suitable substitution.

Variation: For **Baked Chicken** *Empanadas,* substitute 3 ounces cooked chicken or about 1 chicken breast for tuna, and add $1/2$ cup yellow or white onion. For **Chorizo** *Empanadas,* substitute 3 oz. chorizo for tuna. If you can't find Spanish chorizo, substitute pepperoni or salami, but the taste won't be quite the same. Mexican chorizo is not a good substitution because it isn't made the same way.

Chef Matthew Silverman's Shrimp
Empanadas

Chef Silverman's *empanadas* are a bit fancier than my *empanadas*, and they are so incredibly delicious. He serves them with a spicy mayonnaise.

4 cups all-purpose white flour

4 eggs

1 TB. salt

6 oz. water

½ cup unsalted butter, melted

1 TB. extra-virgin olive oil

1 red bell pepper, finely diced

1 yellow bell pepper, finely diced

1 red onion, finely diced

1 lb. shrimp with shells and veins removed and diced

2 cups grated Manchego cheese

Salt and freshly ground pepper

2 TB. fresh parsley, minced

2 egg yolks

2 TB. freshly squeezed lemon juice

2 TB. smoked Spanish paprika

1½ cups soybean oil

1 egg, whisked for egg wash

4 cups oil, soybean or corn for frying

Yield: 24 *empanadas*
Prep Time: 45 minutes
Cook Time: 20 to 30 minutes
Serving Size: 2 to 3 *empanadas*, plus 1 to 2 teaspoons mayonnaise

1. Place flour, eggs, and salt in a standing mixer with a paddle attachment. Mix until just combined, starting on a low setting so flour doesn't spread. Slowly add water and butter, until a ball forms. You may need to add 1 or 2 more tablespoons water. Texture should be like pizza dough.

2. In a medium-size saucepan over medium-low heat, add olive oil, and cook for 1 minute; add red and yellow peppers and onion. *Sweat* or cook vegetables for just 2 to 3 minutes.

3. Add shrimp and cook another 2 or 3 minutes until shrimp just turns pink. Mix with cheese, salt, pepper, and parsley, and chill until ready to fill.

4. Place egg yolks, lemon juice, and paprika into a blender and blend on high a few seconds. With the blender on high, slowly drizzle in soybean oil, a little at a time. Season with salt and pepper.

5. To assemble *empanadas*, roll out dough until $^1/_{16}$-inch thick. Cut out 3-inch circles. Place 1 teaspoon shrimp filling in center of each circle. Fold over dough, and crimp edges together with a fork. Brush dough with egg wash. Note: some dough will be leftover.

6. Heat oil in a deep fryer or a deep pot to 375°F. Add *empanadas*, a few at a time; don't crowd the fryer. Cook for about 5 minutes or until golden brown. Serve with smoked paprika sauce.

⌐Hablo Tapas _____

To **sweat,** in cooking terms, is sort of like sweating, in general. Basically, you just want to cook vegetables over low heat long enough to release their moisture and flavor. Sweating is actually a delicate way to cook.

Arroz Frito with Saffron Alioli or Paella Rice Balls with Saffron Mayonnaise

When Chef Matthew Silverman, executive chef of Vintner Grill and Agave restaurants in Las Vegas, was invited to cook at the James Beard House in New York City, he wanted to do anything but the ordinary so he decided to take a Spanish classic and serve it up in a novel way.

2 cups Arborio rice

2½ cups water

Pinch saffron

1 cup fresh peas, blanched or frozen peas

½ cup Fra'Mani chorizo, finely diced (Fra'Mani is a brand of sausage made by Paul Bertolli from Chez Panisse)

3 eggs

1 cup Manchego cheese, grated

2 TB. parsley, minced

6 cups corn or soybean oil for frying

Saffron Alioli (recipe follows)

Yield: 30 rice balls
Prep Time: 30 minutes
Chill Time: 30 minutes
Cook Time: 8 minutes per batch; 30 minutes total
Serving Size: 2 rice balls

1. Place rice, water, and saffron into a large pot. Cook, uncovered, over medium heat for about 15 minutes. Let cool for 30 minutes.

2. Mix rice with peas, chorizo, eggs, cheese, and parsley. Form into balls.

3. Heat oil in a large pot or deep fryer until 375°F. Fry rice balls until crisp or about 8 minutes. Serve with Saffron Alioli Sauce.

Appetizing Extras

Paella is probably the most well-known Spanish dish and is most often served on the eastern and southern coasts of Spain. Besides chorizo, it often features chicken, fish, and seafood. To properly make paella in Spain, chefs use a paella pan, a big, two-handled dish.

Saffron Alioli or Saffron Mayonnaise

Saffron is always used with paella so it is fitting that Chef Matthew Silverman serves up his paella balls with saffron mayonnaise.

Pinch saffron

¼ cup hot water

2 egg yolks

2 TB. freshly squeezed lemon juice

1½ cups soybean oil

Salt and freshly ground pepper

Yield: 1½ cups mayonnaise

Prep Time: 15 minutes

Serving Size: About 1 tablespoon mayonnaise

1. Steep saffron in hot water for about 2 minutes to release its flavor. Cool for 10 minutes.

2. Place water in a blender with egg yolks and lemon juice, and blend on high. Drizzle in oil, a little bit at a time. Season with salt and pepper, and serve with rice balls.

Gambas al Ajillo

Sort of like Spanish shrimp scampi, this garlic shrimp dish is delicious and deliciously simple.

2 TB. extra-virgin olive oil

3 cloves garlic, minced

12 medium to large size shrimp, with shells and veins removed

4 TB. sherry wine

Juice of ½ lemon

Pinch paprika

Pinch oregano

Salt and pepper

Yield: 12 individual shrimp

Prep Time: 5 minutes

Cook Time: 5 minutes

Serving Size: 3 to 4 shrimp

1. Heat a skillet over medium-high heat for 1 to 2 minutes. Add olive oil and heat for 1 minute. Add garlic and shrimp, and sauté until shrimp is pink.

2. Add wine and lemon juice and cook for 1 minute. Add paprika, oregano, salt, and pepper. Remove from heat and serve.

Tapas Tricks

For some extra heat, add some sliced chili peppers or chili powder.

Gambas a la Plancha—Grilled Shrimp

This is one of the most popular Spanish tapas dishes. But in Spain, the shrimp are typically cooked whole. I prefer cooking them without any of the extra parts.

¼ cup extra-virgin olive oil

3 cloves garlic, finely minced

1 TB. Spanish dry sherry or white wine

3 TB. lemon juice, freshly squeezed

1 tsp. Spanish paprika

Salt and pepper

1 lb. uncooked, medium to large size shrimp, with veins and all but very end of tail removed

Lemon wedges

Yield: 6 to 8 servings

Marinate Time: 15 minutes

Prep Time: 12 minutes

Cook Time: 10 minutes

Serving Size: 4 shrimp

1. In a large bowl, mix olive oil, garlic, sherry, lemon juice, paprika, salt, and pepper. Toss shrimp into mixture and let marinate 15 minutes.

2. Heat grill to high. Remove shrimp from marinade, but reserve marinade. Grill shrimp for 1 to 2 minutes on each side or until pink, cooking in 2 batches. Place on serving platter.

3. In a small saucepan, stir and cook marinade over medium-high heat for about 4 minutes until it is slightly thickened. Pour marinade into a small bowl, and use as a dipping sauce for shrimp.

4. Before serving, squeeze fresh lemon juice over shrimp. Garnish with extra lemon wedges, and serve with cooked marinade on the side.

Appetizing Extras

This tapas dish begs to be eaten with a glass of sherry on the side. At least, that is how many Spaniards enjoy this popular dish. But if sherry is too sweet or cloying for you, try a crisp glass of white Spanish wine. Or try a Fino, Manzanillo, or Amontillado sherry. They tend to be drier and more refreshing.

Baked Salmon with Sherry

In Spain, this dish is usually made with salt cod. But since salt cod can sometimes be hard to find in grocery stores and since it is not always appetizing to American palettes, I replaced the cod with the more popular salmon.

¼ cup Spanish dry sherry or white wine

3 TB. extra-virgin olive oil

1 TB. lemon juice

3 cloves garlic, minced

2 tsp. Spanish paprika

Salt and pepper

4 (8 oz.) *salmon* filets, skinned and boned

Yield: 4 servings
Marinate Time: 15 minutes
Prep Time: 10 minutes
Cook Time: 15 minutes
Serving Size: 1 filet or half a filet if large

1. In a large bowl, mix sherry, olive oil, lemon juice, garlic, paprika, salt, and pepper. Toss salmon in marinade and let set 15 minutes.

2. Preheat oven to 350°F. Transfer salmon and marinade to an oven-proof casserole dish and cook 15 minutes. Garnish with extra lemon wedges.

⌐Hablo Tapas _____

Salmon is one of those words that is basically the same in Spanish as it is in English. In Spanish, however, there's a delightful little accent on the o: *salmón*.

≪━━━┘

Roasted Pork Tenderloin with Adobo Marinade

Known as *lomo en adobo*, this roasted pork dish typically required a week's worth of marinating. This recipe adapts the marinade but retains the taste.

¼ cup extra-virgin olive oil

¼ cup vinegar, white wine, or sherry vinegar

4 cloves garlic, minced

1 TB. fresh rosemary, plus 2 reserved twigs rosemary

2 tsp. Spanish paprika

2 tsp. dried oregano

1 tsp. dried thyme or 1 TB. fresh thyme

1 tsp. granulated sugar

½ tsp. cinnamon

Salt and pepper

2 lbs. pork tenderloin

Yield: 2 pounds pork loin, about 8 to 10 servings

Marinate Time: At least 2 hours, preferably overnight

Prep Time: 20 minutes

Cook Time: 50 minutes

Serving Size: 2 pieces pork tenderloin

1. In a large bowl, mix olive oil, vinegar, garlic, rosemary, paprika, oregano, thyme, sugar, cinnamon, salt, and pepper. Rub marinade into meat, and marinate at least two hours.

2. Preheat oven to 350°F. Remove meat from marinade and place into a roasting pan. Place rosemary twigs on meat.

3. Roast meat for at least 1 hour or until juicy and only slightly pink in the center. If you use a meat thermometer, follow the directions for cooking pork. When roasted, remove meat from the pan and tent with aluminum foil for 5 to 10 minutes. Serve.

Tapas Tricks

If you are using a meat thermometer, cook pork to a temperature of 160°F to 170°F.

Pork Tenderloin with Sherry

Sherry goes well with almost any meat, but it brings out a sweetness when paired with pork tenderloin.

2 lbs. pork tenderloin, sliced into 1/2 inch medallions

4 cloves garlic, minced finely

1/4 cup yellow or white onion, diced

1 TB. loosely packed, fresh rosemary, minced

Salt and pepper

1/2 cup sherry or white wine

Yield: 6 to 8 servings
Prep Time: 30 minutes
Cook Time: 30 minutes
Serving Size: 2 to 3 pork medallions

Tapas Tricks

Never use cooking sherry or cooking wine—it has spices and salt added and is never the same quality as regular sherry or wine. Use regular wine when you cook.

1. Preheat oven to 350°F. Pound pork until about 1/2 inch thick. Sprinkle garlic, onion, rosemary, salt, and pepper over cutlets.

2. Place pork into a roasting pan lined with foil, and pour sherry over it. Roast for at least 1 hour or until meat is only lightly pink in center.

Calamare is a popular seafood tapas dish, and there are some small restaurants in Spain which only make this dish.

Chef Dan Smith, McCormick & Schmick's

Crostini, or toasted bread, are a type of appetizer that are popular in both Spain and Italy. This pancetta crostini is a more modern twist on a traditional favorite.

Chef Gregg DeRosier, Anaba Tea Room

Chef Gregg DeRosier not only pairs his dishes with cups of tea, but he often uses tea to accent the natural flavors of food, as he does with this Asian Duck Breast served with a broth made with a smoky, black tea.

Chef Gregg DeRosier, Anaba Tea Room

For his invitation to cook at the James Beard House, Vintner's Grill Chef Matthew Silverman chose to make a tapas dinner, including these lamb *albondigas*.

Philip Gross

Paella might be the most well-known dish in Spain, but it is not served as tapas. Vintner's Grill Chef Matthew Silverman, however, converted this classic dish into a tapas by serving it as paella balls.

Philip Gross

Tortilla Español or Spanish tortilla is a traditional tapas dish that is served all over Spain, but the best versions of it are found in the Castilla-La Mancha region of Spain. At the Al Foro Restaurant in Toledo, Spain, it is served with *pisto manchego* or sautéed mixed vegetables.

Jeanette Hurt

Croquettas are fried fritters filled with cheese, ham, chicken, or vegetables in a creamy sauce base. These *croquettas* were served as an appetizer at the El Placete restaurant in Toledo, Spain. El Placete is a historic restaurant that is housed in a building that once was a Moorish palace.

Jeanette Hurt

At Restaurant Divino in Segovia, Spain, Chef David Martinez takes classic Spanish tapas to new levels like he does, pairing this hake fish and mussels with spinach.

John Braun

Salads in Spain are traditionally dressed with just olive oil and vinegar, but sometimes chefs like David Martinez, of Restaurant Divino in Segovia, Spain, take simple Spanish dishes and make them extraordinary, as he does by adding marinated salmon and oranges.

John Braun

Restaurant Divino Chef David Martinez calls this "red pepper ravioli," but instead of using pasta flavored with red pepper, he stuffs actual piquillo peppers with fresh chèvre that has been spiced with vanilla.

John Braun

Tapas can be served as individual courses, and small portions of soup and seafood can be artfully arranged in small bowls, as Restaurant Divino Chef David Martinez does with his creamy cauliflower soup and marinated mussel.

John Braun

Artichokes are one of the most common vegetables used in tapas dishes, and Chef David Martinez bakes artichoke hearts with Manchego cheese.

John Braun

At the Al Foro Restaurant in Toledo, Spain, tapas dishes are artfully arranged on one plate. The *ensalada rusa* is served in miniature portions in small prebaked pie shells, and then various crostini are topped with anchovies and chorizo.

John Braun

Mushrooms are often sautéed with garlic in this classic tapas dish.

Foods from Spain and the Trade Commission of Spain

Quail is sometimes served as a tapas dish, as it is at the restaurant of the Reina Sophia Contemporary Art Museum in Madrid.

John Braun

Manchego cheese and other Spanish cheeses are sometimes served alone as a simple tapas dish.

Foods from Spain and the Trade Commission of Spain

Spanish Meatballs

Known as *albondigas*, meatballs are quite a popular tapas in Spain. Traditionally, pork is used instead of beef, and it is often served with alioli (garlic mayonnaise) or a tomato sauce.

½ lb. ground beef

½ lb. ground pork

2 eggs, whisked

½ cup yellow or white onion, minced

¼ cup breadcrumbs

½ tsp. Spanish paprika

½ tsp. cinnamon, Ceylon cinnamon recommended

Salt and pepper

2 TB. extra-virgin olive oil

Yield: 35 meatballs
Prep Time: 20 minutes
Cook Time: 15 minutes
Serving Size: 5 meatballs

1. In a large bowl, mix together beef, pork, eggs, onion, breadcrumbs, paprika, cinnamon, salt, and pepper. Roll mixture into individual balls, about 1 inch in diameter.

2. Heat skillet over medium-high heat for 1 to 2 minutes. Add 2 tablespoons olive oil and heat for 1 minute. Sauté batches of meatballs until meat is cooked on all sides, turning frequently, about 10 minutes.

Tapas Tricks

Use just plain ground beef if you don't like a mixture of beef and pork.

Simple Tomato Sauce for Spanish Meatballs

My friend Tamara Johnston serves this simple tomato sauce with her Spanish meatballs.

14 oz. diced tomatoes

2 TB. Spanish red wine

1 tsp. extra-virgin olive oil

1 tsp. dried basil

½ tsp. dried thyme

Salt and pepper

Yield: 1½ cups sauce or enough to coat meatballs

Prep Time: 5 minutes

Cook Time: 10 minutes

Serving Size: 1 to 2 tablespoons

1. In a medium saucepan over medium-low heat, combine tomatoes, wine, olive oil, basil, thyme, salt, and pepper. Stir and simmer for 10 minutes.

2. Toss with meatballs and serve while hot.

 Tapas Tricks

Here's a note about using salt. If you use high-quality spices—real Ceylon cinnamon, real Spanish paprika, for example—you may not need any salt at all. One really good source for ordering fresh, real spices is the Spice House, whose website is listed in Appendix B.

Lamb Meatballs with Romanesco Sauce

This is another dish that Chef Matthew Silverman served at the James Beard House in New York City. Lamb, a popular meat in Spain, tastes quite delicious in this tapas.

4 slices white bread

½ cup whole or 2 percent milk

1½ lbs. ground lamb

½ cup pine nuts, toasted

1 cup Idiazabal cheese, grated

1 egg

Salt and freshly ground pepper

3 red bell peppers, roasted, peeled, and seeded

2 Roma tomatoes, roasted

5 garlic cloves

2 TB. Parmesan cheese, grated

¼ cup slivered almonds, toasted

½ tsp. granulated sugar

¼ cup extra-virgin olive oil

Yield: 24 meatballs
Prep Time: 20 minutes
Cook Time: 15 minutes
Serving Size: 2 to 4 meatballs

1. In a large bowl, soak bread in milk. Then add lamb, nuts, cheese, and egg. Season with salt and pepper. Roll into balls about 1¼ oz. or 1 to 2 inches in size.

2. Preheat oven to 400°F. Roast meatballs in a shallow baking dish for 8 to 10 minutes.

3. To make sauce, place peppers, tomatoes, garlic, Parmesan, almonds, and sugar into a blender. Purée on high until smooth about 5 minutes. Then slowly drizzle on olive oil. Add salt and pepper.

4. Place 2 to 4 meatballs on a plate, and spoon on 1 or 2 tablespoons sauce.

Tapas Tricks

Though you can eat it right away, the Romanesco sauce will taste better the longer you let the flavors marinate together. So make the sauce first and let it chill for a time.

Beef Kebobs

This dish has a bit of Moorish influence in the spices. In Spain, kebobs are often made from lean pork, but in Spanish restaurants in the United States, they are often made of beef.

½ cup extra-virgin olive oil

2 cloves garlic, minced

Juice and zest of 1 lemon

1 TB. rosemary, chopped finely

2 tsp. Spanish paprika

½ tsp. cinnamon

½ tsp. cumin

1 lb. lean beef, cut into 1-inch cubes, skewered on wooden skewers

Salt and pepper

Yield: 8 servings
Marinate Time: At least 1 hour
Prep Time: 15 minutes, plus 20 minutes for soaking skewers
Cook Time: 5 minutes for medium-rare
Serving Size: 2 to 3 pieces per person

1. Soak wooden skewers in a shallow dish filled with water for 20 minutes.

2. In a large bowl, mix together olive oil, garlic, lemon juice and zest, rosemary, paprika, cinnamon, and cumin. Toss meat in marinade, and marinate for at least 1 hour.

3. Heat grill to high. Salt and pepper the beef. Place beef onto skewers, and cook until desired doneness, about 2½ minutes on each side for medium-rare, longer for more well-done meat.

Variation: You can also use cubed lamb meat.

Appetizing Extras

Though this dish has its roots in Moorish culture—the Moors ruled Spain for 800 some years—the Moors would never make kebobs the Spanish way, using pork.

Fried Calamari with Orange Alioli

Fried calamari is served throughout Spain. This recipe comes from seafood expert, Chef Dan Smith, of McCormick & Schmick's Restaurant in Milwaukee.

2 lbs. calamari (cleaned and cut in ½" to ¾" rings)

2 egg whites

2 ½ cups flour

½ tsp. kosher salt

½ tsp. black pepper

½ tsp. smoked paprika

2 quarts canola or peanut oil

½ cup mayonnaise

1 TB. canola oil

1 tsp. orange zest

1 tsp. orange juice

Salt and pepper

Yield: 4 to 6 servings

Marinate Time: 10 minutes

Prep Time: 20 minutes

Cook Time: 15 minutes for all batches

Serving Size: ⅛ to ¼ pound portion calamari, plus a few tablespoons sauce

1. Heat oil in a high-sided pot until the temperature reaches 350°F.

2. Put cut calamari into a large bowl, add egg whites, and marinate for 10 minutes. Mix salt, pepper, and paprika with flour. Toss calamari in flour mixture, and shake off excess flour into a strainer.

3. Place oil into a deep fryer and heat. Carefully place calamari into hot oil, and fry 3 to 5 minutes or until golden brown.

4. Mix mayonnaise, oil, orange zest, orange juice, salt, and pepper together.

5. To serve, place calamari on a plate or platter and serve with orange alioli.

 Appetizing Extras

Calamari is spelled *calamare* in Spanish. In Spain, fried calamari is sometimes served on sandwiches.

Croquetas de Jamon or Ham Croquettes

Croquetas are one of the most popular appetizers in Spain. These fried, filled fritters are often made with ham, but you can also use other ingredients, too.

1 cup whole milk

1 slice onion

¼ tsp. whole peppercorns

3 or 4 whole cloves

¼ cup yellow or white onion, minced

2 TB., plus 3 cups extra-virgin olive oil

3 TB. white, unbleached flour

¼ lb ham, Serrano or proscuitto

1 TB. fresh chives, minced

3 cups panko breadcrumbs

3 eggs, beaten

⅛ tsp. Kosher or sea salt

Freshly ground white pepper to taste

> **Yield: About 2 dozen**
> **Prep Time:** 30 minutes
> **Cook Time:** 5 minutes
> **Serving Size:** 2 to 4 *croquetas*

1. In a medium-size saucepan, over medium-high heat, bring milk, onion slice, peppercorns, and cloves to a boil. Turn off, and let sit for 15 minutes. Set aside. After 15 minutes is up, use a slotted spoon to remove the peppercorns, onion, and cloves.

2. In a separate saucepan, over medium-high heat, add 1 TB. olive oil. Heat for 1 minute, then add ¼ cup onions, and sauté until transluscent, about 5 minutes. Add 1 TB. flour, mix together, then add 1 more TB. olive oil and 2 TB. flour.

3. Reduce heat to medium, and slowly whisk in the milk. After it thickens, add ham, chives, salt, pepper, and ½ cup of the breadcrumbs. Set aside and let cool.

4. Lightly flour your hands, and then form the thickened sauce mixture into balls or logs. Roll in breadcrumbs, then dip in egg, then roll in breadcrumbs and set aside.

5. Heat 3 cups of oil up to 370°F in either pan or fryer. In small batches, carefully place *croquetas* into the oil. Cook for about 5 minutes or until golden brown. Drain on paper towels before serving.

6. Serve plain or with Alioli or Lemon *Mayonesa* (recipe in Chapter 3).

Variations: Substitute ham with ¼ lb. of shredded or diced chicken, tuna, cheese, or even cooked vegetables like spinach.

> **Tapas Tricks**
>
> *Croquetas* can be formed into squares, balls, or most popularly, oval-shaped logs. I find that logs are the easiest shape in which to form them.

Creamed Cauliflower with Tomato Soup and Pistachio Nuts

Tapas can go upscale, and this unusual pairing was served to me at the Restaurant Divino in Segovia. It was even more unusual in that it was served with the steamed mussels on the side.

1 head cauliflower, cut into pieces

1 TB. extra-virgin olive oil

1 cup yellow or white onion, finely diced

1 cup half-and-half

Salt and white pepper

5 cups creamy tomato soup

½ cup chopped pistachio nuts

Yield: 5 cups cauliflower and 5 cups tomato soup

Prep Time: 10 minutes

Cook Time: 5 minutes

Serving Size: 1 cup

1. In a vegetable steamer, steam cauliflower for 10 minutes.

2. In a medium-size saucepan over medium-high heat, warm for 1 minute. Add olive oil, and heat for another minute, then sauté onion until translucent, about 3 to 5 minutes.

3. In either a blender or food processor, purée onions, cauliflower, and half-and-half.

4. Heat up puréed cauliflower mixture in pan over medium heat, season with salt and pepper. Warm tomato soup in a separate pot over medium heat.

5. To serve, place about ½ cup of cauliflower mixture in the middle of a bowl, then pour soup around the mixture. Top with a teaspoon or two of pistachio nuts.

 Tapas Tricks

For optimum elegance, serve this dish with individual mussels with Beurre Blanc Sauce.

Steamed Mussels with Beurre Blanc Sauce

This is an upscale tapas dish that was served in conjunction with the creamed cauliflower with tomato soup and pistachios at the Restaurant Divino in Segovia. It is one of the most upscale tapas dishes I have ever enjoyed.

2 dozen fresh mussels

3 TB. shallots, chopped

1 cup sherry

1 cup water

1 recipe Beurre Blanc Sauce, follows

Yield: 2 dozen mussels

Prep Time: 15 minutes

Cook Time: 5 minutes

Serving Size: 1 individual mussel

1. Scrub mussels in cold water using a stiff brush to remove any sand or grit and the "beard," which is a scruffy, plantlike attachment to the mussels. Some beards are easily removed, but others require a knife to cut them off.

2. In a large saucepan over high heat, add the shallots, sherry, water, and mussels and cover with a clear lid. After the mixture begins to boil or steam, cook for 5 minutes or until all the mussels are opened.

3. Serve with broth or Beurre Blanc Sauce.

Variation: Instead of Beurre Blanc Sauce or broth, you can also serve the mussels with ½ cup of pesto.

 Tapas Tricks

For optimum elegance, serve this dish with an individual portion of creamy cauliflower with tomato soup and pistachios.

Beurre Blanc Sauce

This is more of a French sauce, but it can be easily implemented in tapas cooking.

2 tsp. extra-virgin olive oil

2 TB. shallots, finely diced

3 TB. white wine

3 TB. white wine or champagne vinegar

4 TB. unsalted butter, cut into chunks

1 TB. chives, finely chopped

Salt and white pepper to taste

Yield: ⅓ cup
Prep Time: 5 minutes
Cook Time: 15 minutes
Serving Size: 1 to 2 teaspoons

1. In a small pan over medium-high heat, sauté shallots and olive oil for about 2 minutes. Add wine and vinegar, and then cook until reduced by half or for about 5 to 7 minutes.

2. Reduce heat to medium-low and add butter, one chunk at a time. To properly emulsify the sauce, you will be adding a chunk, heating it, then removing it from the heat when it is almost melted. You will add a chunk, then heat, and then remove from heat, stirring almost constantly.

3. When the butter is completely melted and combined, add the chives, salt, and pepper. Serve over shellfish or fish.

Variation: You can make a **Red Beurre Blanc Sauce** by using red wine and red wine vinegar. To make a more **Traditional Beurre Blanc Sauce,** use tarragon instead of chives.

Tapas Tricks

Beurre blanc sauces traditionally are served with fish and shellfish, but it also can be used to top chicken breasts.

Whitefish and Spinach Topped with Mussels

At the Restaurant Divino in Segovia, this dish was made with hake, a type of cod, but you can use regular cod. I have also made this dish with other white-fleshed fish like tilefish.

Salt and pepper to taste

4 filets of cod or other fish, de-boned and skin removed

1 TB. extra-virgin olive oil

4 cups cooked fresh spinach

1 batch Beurre Blanc Sauce (recipe in this chapter)

1 batch Steamed Individual Mussels (recipe in this chapter)

Yield: 4 filets
Prep Time: 20 minutes
Cook Time: 10 minutes
Serving Size: 1 filet

1. Salt and pepper filets. Set aside.

2. Heat a large saucepan over high heat for 1 to 2 minutes. Add olive oil and heat for another 2 minutes. Add filets. Cook each filet for about 2 to 3 minutes per side.

3. To serve, place one cup of spinach on plate, top with filet. Then top with 3 to 4 individual mussels, removed from their shells. Spoon 2 to 3 teaspoons of Beurre Blanc Sauce on top.

Variation: Instead of mussels, serve with cooked shrimp or scallops.

 Tapas Tricks _____

For added eye appeal, sprinkle extra herbs over and around each plate.

Chapter 10

International Tapas Dishes

In This Chapter

◆ Indian and Asian tapas

◆ South American and Mexican tapas

◆ European tapas

Perhaps one sign of tapas's growing popularity is the expansion of tapas from traditional Spanish restaurants and dishes to the international realm. Tapas, from Filipino egg rolls to Chilean *empanadas*, are taking the world by storm.

Almost every culture has little bites, appetizers, or hors d'oeuvres on its menus. But whereas appetizers may have always been a traditional part of many cuisines, today both professional and home chefs quite often combine different aspects of different cuisines and create new dishes.

This chapter explores some fusion dishes—the combination of two or more different cuisines—as well as other, traditional appetizers from around the globe. International tapas dishes can be great for parties, and it's fun to mix and match different dishes together.

Filipino Fusion Egg Rolls

Egg rolls are just one of those absolutely delightful appetizers. Although they require a bit of assembly, they're worth the work.

1 lb. lean ground beef

½ cup diced yellow or white onion

1 clove garlic, minced

4 leaves napa cabbage, about 1½ cups, julienned into 4-inch long pieces

½ cup green onions, chopped

½ cup bamboo shoots, cut into matchstick-thin pieces

½ cup carrots, cut into matchstick-thin pieces

½ cup bean sprouts

½ cup water chestnuts, chopped

¼ lb. cooked, medium shrimp, with veins and tails removed, chopped

4 TB. soy sauce

2 TB. cilantro, finely chopped

1 TB. fresh ginger, minced

2 tsp. granulated sugar

Pinch cayenne pepper

1 (12 oz. package) spring roll wrappers

1 egg, beaten for wash

6 cups canola oil

Yield: 25 egg rolls
Prep Time: 2 hours
Cook Time: 20 minutes
Serving Size: 2 to 3 egg rolls

1. Heat a large saucepan over medium-high heat. Add beef and cook for about 4 minutes. Add white onion and garlic and cook for 3 more minutes.

2. Add cabbage, bamboo, carrots, bean sprouts, green onions, and water chestnuts, and cook for 2 minutes. Then add shrimp, soy sauce, cilantro, ginger, sugar, and cayenne. Cook for 2 more minutes, then remove from heat.

3. If using unrefrigerated spring roll wrappers, wet each individual wrapper with medium-hot water first so that it is flexible enough to fold.

4. To assemble, place 1¹/₂ tablespoons mixture in a narrow line on wrapper, about 1 inch from top. Gently fold over top of wrapper, tuck in sides, and wrap until entire wrapper is folded. Brush with egg wash to seal.

5. Heat oil to 375°F in either a large pot or a deep fryer. Fry, turning occasionally, for about 10 minutes or until crisp. Serve with sweet-and-sour sauce or hot mustard.

Tapas Tricks

Because Filipino egg rolls are longer and thinner than regular egg rolls, spring roll wrappers, which are typically larger than egg roll wrappers, and are easier to use. If you have access to a good Asian grocery, they might sell frozen or refrigerated wrappers, which are ready to use. Spring roll wrappers that are not refrigerated must be softened by soaking or running warm water over them first.

Three Cheese Tartlets with Lingonberry Jam

Cheese and berries go together almost as well as peanut butter and jelly. These little tartlets dress up any appetizer plate, and they're so good that it's hard to stop eating them.

1 tsp. extra-virgin olive oil

1 cup yellow or white onions, minced

2 prepared piecrusts or about 15 oz.

3 eggs

8 oz. mascarpone cheese

4 oz. fresh goat cheese or chèvre, crumbled

4 oz. Swiss or blue cheese, grated or crumbled

1 cup lingonberry jam

Yield: 40 tartlets

Prep Time: 15 minutes

Cook Time: 15 minutes

Serving Size: 3 to 4 tartlets

1. Heat a medium saucepan over medium-high heat 1 minute. Add olive oil; heat 1 minute; add onions; and sauté until caramelized, about 3 minutes.

2. Preheat oven to 375°F. Cut piecrusts into 40 squares or circles, about 2 inches in diameter. You will not use all of the second piecrust. Place piecrusts into a nonstick mini muffin tin using a wooden dowel or your fingers to press into the sides and just above the pan.

3. Whisk eggs, mascarpone, goat cheese, and either Swiss or blue cheese together.

4. Place $^1/_2$ teaspoon caramelized onion into bottom of each tartlet. Spoon about 1 tablespoon cheese and egg mixture onto onion. Then top each with about $^1/_2$ teaspoon jam.

5. Bake tartlets for 15 minutes or until they puff up a bit and are golden on top. Serve immediately.

Variation: For variety, use apricot or raspberry jam.

Homemade Guacamole

Homemade guacamole is just about as easy as using dry guacamole mixes, but the taste is so much better. Serve this with tortilla chips or the home-made plantain chip recipe that follows.

2 ripe avocados

1 medium-size tomato

½ cup yellow or white onion, chopped

⅓ cup cilantro, minced

1 jalapeño, seeded and pith removed

Juice of 1 lime

Salt and pepper

> **Yield: 1 cup of guacamole**
>
> **Prep Time:** 5 minutes
>
> **Serving Size:** 2 to 3 tablespoons

1. Place avocados, tomato, onion, cilantro, jalapeño, and lime juice into a food processor fitted with a standard chopping blade or a blender. Process on high for about 3 minutes.

2. Add salt and pepper. Serve with chips or fried plantains.

 Tapas Tricks

A shortcut to good guacamole is to combine 1 cup mild or medium salsa with two avocados in a blender. It's not quite as good as using all fresh ingredients, but it is much better than the guacamole seasoning.

Fried Plantain Chips

Fried plantains are a staple of Puerto Rican and Cuban cuisine, often served with black beans and rice. But when they're thinly sliced and fried, they make a delicious alternative to tortilla chips.

3 plantains, not too ripe

6 cups canola oil

1 tsp. salt

Yield: 2½ to 3 cups chips

Prep Time: 15 minutes

Cook Time: 10 minutes

Serving Size: ½ cup

1. Peel plantains. Using a mandolin or a vegetable peeler, cut into very, very thin strips or pieces.

2. Heat oil in a large pot or deep fryer to 375°F. Fry chips in small batches for about 10 minutes per batch.

3. Drain on paper towels. Sprinkle with salt and serve.

Appetizing Extras

Many large grocery stores sell fried plantain chips in the Mexican or Latino foods aisle. But bagged chips never taste quite as good as homemade.

Asparagus Beef Tridents

Filet mignon is always good and is especially delicious in this elegant appetizer.

1 (12 to 14 oz.) *filet mignon*

1 TB. Dijon mustard

½ tsp. horseradish

¼ tsp. honey

Salt and pepper

16 asparagus spears, ends trimmed and blanched or quickly steamed and still crisp

⅛ cup extra-virgin olive oil

Yield: 6 appetizers
Prep Time: 20 minutes
Cook Time: 5 minutes
Serving Size: 1 trident

1. Cut filet into a spiral, from outside in to create one long strip (to save time, you can ask your butcher to do this for you).

2. Whisk mustard, horseradish, and honey. Sprinkle salt and pepper on beef strip. Cut beef into 6 equal-size pieces, about 3 to 4 inches long. Spread mustard mix on top of each.

3. Place 3 asparagus spears across strip of beef, and roll beef secure with bamboo skewer.

4. Brush skewers with olive oil (you will not use up all of the olive oil).

5. Preheat grill to high. Place skewers on the grill, and grill for about 5 minutes or to desired doneness, turning twice so that each is properly seared. Serve with horseradish sauce (recipe follows).

⌐Hablo Tapas

Filet mignon is a French term, which means small boneless meat. It is sometimes referred to as tenderloin steak.

Horseradish Sauce

This is my friend Karen Mahliot's special sauce for beef, and it goes perfectly with the beef tridents.

½ cup heavy cream

1 TB. prepared horseradish

Yield: ½ cup
Prep Time: 5 minutes
Serving Size: About 1 tablespoon

1. Whip cream. Whisk in horseradish and serve.

Appetizing Extras

This sauce is great as a topping for regular steaks and even pork tenderloin. You can also mix the sauce into mashed potatoes for a special kick.

Grilled Ginger Shrimp

Ginger is often used in Asian, especially Thai, cuisine, and it adds a touch of spicy sweetness to any dish.

28 medium shrimp, raw, pealed and vein removed

2 tsp. fresh ginger, finely grated

1 TB. extra-virgin olive oil

Salt

Yield: 4 servings
Prep Time: 10 minutes
Cook Time: 5 minutes
Serving Size: Skewer with 4 shrimp

1. Heat grill to high. Skewer shrimp, 4 to a skewer. Sprinkle with salt.
2. Whisk ginger and olive oil, and brush on shrimp.

3. Grill until pink on each side or about 2 minutes per side. Serve with sweet-and-sour sauce.

Variation: Mix 1 to 2 teaspoons fresh grated ginger with 1 cup prepared sweet-and-sour sauce to serve on the side with the shrimp.

Tapas Tricks

If you double-skewer the shrimp—with one skewer on each side of the shrimp—it will be easier to turn them on the grill; single-skewered shrimp tend to spin around on the skewers.

Indian Scallops Beggar Bags

My friend Ranjana Patnaik is an amazing cook, who often combines Indian cuisine with French. This is one of her delicious concoctions.

1 package phyllo dough (15 sheets)

4 TB. unsalted butter, melted

½ lb. bay scallops, the small kind

1 green onion, minced

1 Serrano chili, seeded and minced

2 TB. fresh cilantro, minced

28 medium shrimp, raw, pealed, and veins removed

1 to 2 tsp. lime zest

¼ tsp. curry powder

Yield: 6 servings
Prep Time: 30 minutes
Cook Time: 20 minutes
Serving Size: 1 beggar's bag

1. Preheat oven to 350°F. Cut 15 phyllo dough sheets in half (each sheet has 5 layers). Lay one half sheet on a flat surface. Brush with melted butter, and place second sheet turned at a 35° angle. Repeat until you have a stack of 5 sheets looking like a flower. Repeat with all sheets.

2. Mix together scallops, onion, chili, cilantro, shrimp, lime zest, and curry.

3. Place ⅙ mixture, about 2 teaspoons, in center of each flower. Pull dough gently around filling, and pinch into a bag with petals spreading out. (If you want to get fancy, tie with blanched chive or green onion strip.) Brush outside of bag with butter.

4. Bake for 20 minutes or until petals turn golden brown.

Variation: Use chicken instead of shrimp.

> **Tapas Tricks**
>
> If the petal tips are browning too quickly, place a sheet of aluminum foil over them.

Salmon Jerky Crostini

Crostini is one of those delicious Italian appetizers, but this dish adds a touch of the Pacific Northwest. It is simple but delicious.

1 loaf French bread

1 avocado

Juice of 1 lime

16 oz. caramelized salmon jerky, often sold in fish markets, sliced into small pieces

3 TB. chives, minced

Yield: 8 to 10 servings
Prep Time: 15 minutes
Cook and Assembly Time: 10 minutes
Serving Size: 2 crostinis

1. Preheat broiler to low.

2. Cut bread into thin, diagonal slices. Cut avocado into thin strips, and put into a bowl. Sprinkle avocado with lime juice.

> **Tapas Tricks**
>
> If you can't find smoked salmon jerky, substitute with regular smoked salmon.

3. Toast bread in broiler until it is golden brown about 2 minutes. Place avocado strip on bread piece, top with salmon jerky slice. Sprinkle with chives and serve.

Tropical Mango Greens Salad

Mango adds a sweet, Latin touch to salads and not just salads made of fruit.

2 mangos, cut into small pieces

4 tsp. fresh cilantro, minced

4 cups mixed greens

¼ cup freshly squeezed lime juice

¼ cup balsamic vinegar

⅔ cup extra-virgin olive oil

1 green onion, minced

Salt and fresh ground pepper

Yield: 4 servings
Prep Time: 10 minutes
Cook Time: 5 minutes
Serving Size: 1 cup greens, topped with mango pieces and dressing

1. Toss mangos, cilantro, and greens together.

2. Whisk lime juice, vinegar, olive oil, onion, salt, and pepper.

3. Toss salad with dressing, and divide evenly among 4 plates.

Appetizing Extras

Although most mangos are imported to the United States from Central and South America, mangos actually originated in Southeast Asia about 4,000 years ago.

Pancetta Crostini

Chef Gregg DeRosier, of the Anaba Tea Room, makes a variety of delicious, little sandwiches, and this sumptuous canapé not only makes a great tapas selection, but it also goes well when served with either a pinot gris or a pinot noir.

4 cloves garlic, minced

4 oz. fresh watercress

3 TB. honey

4 oz. goat cheese

4 thick slices pancetta ham, about 4 to 6 oz.

4 slices whole-grain or whole-wheat bread, toasted with crusts removed and cut on a diagonal

1 Roma tomato, preferably organic

Pinch smoked sea salt

Yield: 4 servings
Prep Time: 15 minutes
Cook and Assembly Time: 10 minutes
Serving Size: 1 open-face sandwich

1. Preheat oven to 375°F.

2. In a food processor fitted with a standard chopping blade, purée garlic, watercress, honey, and goat cheese. Mix until smooth.

3. Cook pancetta until crisp, 8 to 10 minutes.

4. To assemble, spoon goat cheese mixture onto toast points. Stand pancetta in goat cheese and lay tomato slice next to cheese mixture; sprinkle tomato with sea salt.

 Tapas Tricks

If you can't find smoked sea salt, regular sea salt is almost as good.

Asian Duck with Tea Sauce

Chef Gregg DeRosier, of the Anaba Tea Room, makes a variety of delicious appetizers often infused with tea. This tapas is infused with a smoked, black tea.

1 (4 oz.) duck breast

1 TB. chili paste

6 oz. strong lapsang souchong tea (a smoked black tea)

20 oz. beef broth

20 oz. mushroom broth

20 oz. vegetable broth

1 tsp. tumeric

1 cup short-grain rice, cooked with chicken broth

2 oz. shredded cabbage (about ¼ cup)

1 carrot, cut into thin julienne slices

1 green onion, thinly sliced lengthwise

½ cup mushrooms (White Beech recommended)

Watercress leaves for garnish

Yield: 4 servings
Prep Time: 30 minutes
Cook and Assembly Time: 10 minutes
Serving Size: 1 assembled duck breast

1. Rub duck with chili paste, coating entire breast. Heat a skillet to medium-high heat. Fry breast, first skin up. Cook 4 minutes, turn and cook skin side 3 minutes. Turn the heat off, but leave the pan on the burner.

2. Bring tea and beef, mushroom, and vegetable broth to a rolling boil, and turn off heat.

3. Mix tumeric into rice.

4. To assemble, lay bed of cabbage in a small bowl; add carrots, onion, mushrooms, and warm rice. Slice duck into 8 thin pieces, and lay 2 pieces over each portion of rice and vegetables.

5. Serve each portion with a small cup of broth. You will have a lot of broth left over. The chef recommends pairing with chopsticks and sake. You can use the leftover broth to make a savory soup like French onion or cream of mushroom (12-oz. package).

Tapas Tricks _____

Lapsang souchong tea is a common tea found in tea shops but also can be ordered online.

Part 4

The Good Life: Sweets, Drinks, and Party Tips

Wow! We've covered a lot of ground, and by now, we've spent quite a bit of time in the kitchen. But we're not quite finished yet. These three chapters complete your tapas experience as we cover sweets and desserts, along with Spanish wine and sangria. We even explore tips for hosting your own Spanish tapas party.

Chapter **11**

Dulces

In This Chapter

- ◆ Flan and Spanish custards
- ◆ Cookies and cakes
- ◆ Chocolate

Desserts aren't really tapas dishes, but no tapas meal is complete without a delicious, sweet, Spanish dessert. In Spain, after a heavy meal, people like to linger with a cup of *café con leche* or a glass of sweet sherry with a decadent treat.

Some Spanish desserts are simple, homey affairs like rice pudding or *arroz con leche*. Others are more complicated, like flan or baked custard with caramel sauce. As with many Spanish dishes, cinnamon and either lemon or orange peel are favorite flavors. Even olive oil is sometimes used as a dessert ingredient.

If you are serving a tapas meal and want to finish it off right, serve small portions. But unlike the tapas meal itself, which involves many small dishes and savory bites, you don't have to serve more than one dessert at a time.

Sherry Almond Cake

This is a simplified version of a Spanish cake known as "drunken cake," also known as *borrachos*.

1 (18.25 oz.) package yellow cake mix

1 cup chopped almonds

3 eggs

1 (4 oz.) package instant vanilla pudding (4-serving size)

½ cup unsalted butter

¾ cup sugar

½ cup sherry wine (sweet sherry)

½ tsp. cinnamon

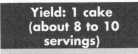

Yield: 1 cake (about 8 to 10 servings)

Prep Time: 15 minutes

Bake Time: 1 hour

Serving Size: One slice

1. Preheat oven to 325°F. Grease and flour a 12-cup bundt cake pan or 10-inch tube pan. Mix cake mix, almonds, eggs, and pudding together.

2. Bake for 1 hour or until a toothpick inserted comes out clean. Remove and cool for 30 minutes.

3. Make glaze by melting butter in saucepan. Add sugar, sherry, and cinnamon. Cook about 10 minutes, until warmed and slightly reduced.

4. Poke holes in cake, and pour glaze over top. Serve dusted with powdered sugar.

Hablo Tapas

The direct translation for the name of this cake, *borrachos*, does not mean "drunken cake" exactly. In Spanish, *borracho* means drunk, and *borrachos* is the plural form of the adjective. But I think the cake term means if you eat too much of this cake, you will become inebriated.

Almond Sugar Cookies

Almond sugar cookies are popular cookies throughout Spain. This is sort of a kicked-up-a-notch sugar cookie recipe.

1 cup unsalted butter, cut into inch-size pieces and room temperature

1 cup granulated sugar plus more for decoration

2 eggs

1 tsp. vanilla or almond extract

3 cups white, unbleached flour, sifted

1 TB. lemon zest

1 tsp. baking soda

¼ tsp. salt

1 tsp. cream of tartar

¼ cup slivered almonds

Yield: 42 cookies
Prep Time: 50 minutes
Bake Time: 10 minutes
Serving Size: 2 to 3 cookies

1. Preheat oven to 350°F. Mix butter and sugar together until well blended. Add eggs, vanilla, flour, zest, baking soda, salt, and cream of tartar. Mix until well blended.

2. Roll cookie dough into 1-inch balls. Roll balls in sugar, and press onto nonstick or greased cookie sheet, using the back of a glass. Press slivered almonds into cookies.

3. Bake for 9 to 10 minutes. Cool on a rack for at least 10 minutes before serving.

Appetizing Extras

The United States is the world's largest producer of almonds, accounting for 68 percent of almond production, but Spain is the second largest producer, accounting for about 16 percent of the world's production.

Arroz con Leche or Rice Pudding

One of the most popular desserts in Spain, this is very simple to make.

1½ cups short-grain rice, like Arborio

2½ cups water

4 tsp. ground cinnamon

1 tsp. lemon zest

5 cups whole milk

¾ cup granulated sugar

Whipped cream

> **Yield: 10 servings**
>
> **Prep Time:** 5 minutes
>
> **Cook Time:** 60 minutes
>
> **Set Time:** 5 minutes
>
> **Serving Size:** 4 oz.

1. Over medium-high heat in a saucepan, cook rice, water, 2 teaspoons cinnamon, and lemon zest. Bring to a boil, cover, and cook over low heat until water is absorbed, about 5 to 10 minutes. Rinse rice with cool water, and set aside.

2. In a medium saucepan over medium-high heat, bring milk, 2 teaspoons cinnamon, and sugar to the point of scalding, just enough to melt the sugar and to foam it; it will take about 15 minutes.

3. Add rice to milk, reduce heat to medium or medium-low, and cook about 15 minutes or until rice is soft and mixture has a somewhat soupy texture. Stir frequently with a wooden spoon or spatula to prevent the bottom of the pan from scorching.

4. Let set for 5 minutes, and spoon into serving bowls. Serve topped with whipped cream.

Tapas Tricks

Instead of cooking the rice in a saucepan, you can cook it in a rice cooker. The only difference is to follow the cooking time on the rice cooker.

Flan or Baked Custard with Caramel Sauce

Flan is such a popular dessert in Spanish restaurants that you might even find flan mixes in Spanish grocery stores. My husband and his sister enjoyed flan while they lived in Puerto Rico, and this is her recipe for recreating their favorite desert.

3 cups sugar

2 large eggs

2 egg yolks

1 (7 oz.) can evaporated milk

1 (7 oz.) can sweetened condensed milk

⅓ cup heavy cream

2 tsp. vanilla extract

⅛ tsp. anise extract

2 TB. vanilla spice rum

Whipping cream (optional)

Yield: 8 servings
Prep Time: 30 minutes
Cook Time: 1 hour
Chill Time: 30 minutes
Serving Size: 1 ramekin or custard dish

1. Preheat oven to 350°F. Set out eight small (about 4 oz. size) ramekins or custard dishes.

2. Place 2 cups sugar in a heavy-bottomed saucepan over medium-low heat. As it begins to liquefy and bubble, swirl the pot to ensure even browning and stir constantly. Remove from heat when sugar is the color of light molasses, about 10 minutes.

3. Use a small metal ladle to put about 2 tablespoons caramel into each ramekin. Turn and rock ramekin while caramel is still liquid, coating sides. Cool completely before filling with custard.

4. To make custard, whisk eggs and yolks just enough to combine; do not overbeat. Stir in 1 cup sugar, and let mixture rest until all bubbles disappear.

5. In a separate bowl, combine evaporated milk, condensed milk, cream, vanilla, anise, and rum. Gently stir this into egg mixture, and let it rest until sugar dissolves. Stir gently again, and ladle into prepared ramekins.

6. Fill a deep roasting pan about halfway up with warm water to create a *bain marie*. Place ramekins ²/₃ deep into water. Bake about 1 hour at 350°F or until custards are set. Remove when custards are loose enough to jiggle in the center when tapped or shaken. The center will be slightly wobbly, but if you touch it in the center with your finger, when you lift it off, there will be no custard on your finger.

7. Cool at least 30 minutes. To serve, run a thin knife around the edge of each ramekin and invert onto plate. Serve with whipped cream if desired.

Hablo Tapas

A **bain marie** is a cooking technique in which one dish containing food is placed inside another, larger pan holding water. This gentle procedure of cooking protects the delicate custard from the oven's heat thanks to the water bath surrounding it.

Crème Catalan

This dessert is sort of like Spain's version of crème brûlée. But unlike crème brûlée, it is infused with lemon or orange and cinnamon.

2 cups whole milk

2 small pieces lemon rind

1 TB. vanilla extract

¹/₂ teaspoon cinnamon

6 egg yolks

1 cup plus 4 TB. sugar

¹/₂ teaspoon cornstarch

Yield: 4 servings
Prep and Infusion Time: 15 minutes
Cook Time: 15 minutes
Refrigerate Time: 1 to 2 hours

1. In a medium saucepan over medium-high heat, bring milk to a simmer and turn off heat. Add lemon rind, vanilla, and cinnamon. Let stand for 10 minutes. Remove lemon rind.

2. In a separate bowl, beat egg yolks and 1 cup sugar. Over low to medium heat, begin heating infused milk and slowly mix in egg yolks, whisking a little at a time. Add cornstarch and cook until thickened, about 15 minutes.

3. Pour into ramekins or small custard dishes, and chill for at least 1 hour.

4. Before serving, sprinkle 1 tablespoon sugar over each dish. Heat broiler. Let sugar caramelize for 1 to 2 minutes. Serve plain, or garnish with whipped cream.

Tapas Tricks _____

If you don't want to use your broiler, add just a little bit of prepared caramel sauce on top of the crèmes. It's not as authentic, but it still tastes great.

Spanish Hot Chocolate

Sipping this sweet treat is almost like drinking liquid pudding—it is that rich, and it is that decadent.

12 oz. bittersweet chocolate

8 oz. unsweetened chocolate

2 cups whole milk

2 cups half-and-half

½ cup granulated sugar

2 tsp. vanilla extract

Yield: 6 cups
Prep and Infusion Time: 15 minutes
Cook Time: 15 minutes
Refrigerate Time: 1 to 2 hours
Serving Size: ½ cup

1. In a medium saucepan over medium-low heat, melt bittersweet and unsweetened chocolate.

2. After chocolate is almost melted, add milk, half-and-half, sugar, and vanilla. Cook until heated and warm but not simmering, about 5 minutes.

3. Serve with a dollop of whipped cream, cookies, or churros.

Variation: For an extra kick, add 2 teaspoons cinnamon or nutmeg. Or add 2 teaspoons orange or coffee liquor in addition to the cinnamon or nutmeg.

Appetizing Extras

Spanish Hot Chocolate is often served with churros or cylindrically shaped donuts.

Chapter 12

¡Salud!: Spanish Wine, Sangria, and More

In This Chapter

- ◆ History of Spanish wine
- ◆ Spanish wines you must try
- ◆ Spanish sherry
- ◆ Pairing wine with tapas
- ◆ Sangria and other drink recipes

Vino or wine is an important part of Spanish history and culture and an equally important part of its cuisine. In Spain, wine accompanies many meals, and no tapas meal is complete without a nice glass of wine or sangria to complement it. If you are not a big fan of wine, Spain offers other drinks to complete your meal nicely, like a good beer or hard cider. This chapter not only explores the wines of Spain but also addresses pairing Spanish wines with tapas. And, of course, it includes recipes for Spain's most famous wine punch, sangria.

Some Wine Background

Spain is, indeed, one of the world's largest cultivators of the vine. At last count, it was second only to France in overall wine production, just slipping in front of Italy and ahead of the United States. In terms of overall landmass dedicated to viticulture, Spain has 1.2 million hectares of land covered by vineyards, with only grains and olive trees taking up more agricultural space.

What's really exciting, though, is that more and more Spanish wines are becoming available in the United States. That's good news for Spanish food aficionados, as nothing quite complements Spanish food like a good Spanish *vino*.

A Brief History of Spanish *Vino*

Spanish wine is the result of many influences over thousands of years. Wine production on the *Iberian Peninsula* (Spain and Portugal) dates back to the time of the ancient Phoenicians and Greeks, who set up colonies there. When the Romans came a conquering in the first century B.C.E., wine production was pretty well established.

> **Hablo Tapas**
>
> The **Iberian Peninsula** is the most southern peninsula in Europe and the landmass that encompasses Spain and Portugal. It is bordered by the Pyrenees Mountains to the north, the Atlantic Ocean to the west, and the Mediterranean Sea to the east and south.

Wine production continued to flourish until the eighth century when the Moors moved into Spain. Because the Koran prohibited the consumption of alcohol, winemaking slowed while the Arabs ruled the country. But after the reconquest of Spain (from 722 to 1492), Catholic monks revived winemaking traditions.

A wine blight in the nineteenth century destroyed many vineyards throughout Europe, primarily in France. Many winemakers who had lost their vineyards moved to Spain and were responsible for establishing some cabernet sauvignon and merlot vineyards that still produce wine today.

Toward the end of the nineteenth century, the phylloxera, the blight causing bugs, made their way to Spain. Fortunately, however, the country did not suffer as much as the rest of Europe thanks to a graphing method that graphed European vines to American rootstock. This kept the bugs away and the wine flowing.

During the twentieth century, the Spanish wine industry experienced some quality reforms but also some setbacks. The Spanish Civil War and World War II left some vineyards pretty beat up, but by the 1950s and 1960s, the wine industry recovered and was modernized.

But things really started getting exciting in the '70s and '80s when some winemakers introduced New World winemaking techniques, pairing them with the traditional, centuries-old grapes. Today, the Spanish wine industry is thriving, and Spain is exporting more and more wines.

Appetizing Extras

One of the most recent—and interesting—developments in the Spanish wine industry is that Spain now makes ice wine. The ultra-sweet dessert wine is made when the grapes freeze on the vine before they are pressed. Because Spain's more temperate climate doesn't allow for that, they make the wine by partially freezing the grapes.

Three Important Wine Regions to Know

Since joining the European Union, the Spanish government has set up an extensive system of wine regions or *Denominacion de Origin* (D.O.) classifications, similar to those of Italy and France. Because there are more than 50 separate and distinct regions, to detail each one in this short chapter would be impossible. Instead, let's take a look at three of the more well-known regions, Rioja, Ribera del Duero, and the sherry producing Jerez.

Rioja, located in north central Spain, is named for the River, or *Rio*, Oja that runs through it; thus the name, Rioja. This region has a long history of making quality wines, and in fact, as far back as 1560, regional winemakers banded together to set up a control board to ensure quality. Rioja makes both red and white wines, and the red Rioja bottles come from a blend of grapes that start with the base of the tempranillo grape.

Perhaps Rioja's biggest rival region is Ribera del Duero, which some oenophiles (wine lovers) describe as the most exciting wine region in the country. Located just north of Madrid in central Spain, this region boasts not only tempranillo grapes but also merlot and cabernet sauvignon grapes, which are blended into these bold red wines.

Appetizing Extras

Wine writer Leslie Sbrocco describes Rioja wines as "the vinous version of Antonio Banderas: spicy, smooth, and sexy."

Another very important wine region is Jerez or the sherry wine region. Sherry wine is a fortified wine because extra alcohol, usually in the form of brandy, is added to it during the winemaking process. Wine has been made in this corner of lower Andalusia for thousands of years.

Spanish Wines and Wine Classification

Classifying wines can get a little confusing because of the many ways used to differentiate them. The types of containers they are stored in during fermentation, the length of fermentation, and the types of grapes used are just a few classifying elements.

Wine Categories

While Spain's regions may be a bit cumbersome to explore, the wines themselves are easy to understand and enjoy. The first step to understanding Spanish wine is to know the four main categories of wines: *joven, crianza, reserva,* and *gran reserva.*

Joven, which means young in Spanish, wines are young, fresh wines, typically made in stainless steel tanks and released the year after they are made. Fruity and lively, they're easy to drink. *Crianza* wines are aged at least two years, and at least one year of aging has to happen in an oak barrel. They have a much richer flavor than *joven* wines.

Reserva wines are aged for three years, with one year in a barrel. Finally, *gran reserva* wines are made from only exceptional vintages and spend two years in oak and three years in the bottle before they are released. Both *reserva* and especially *gran reserva* have deep, rich flavors—they are the kind of wines that make you swoon.

Reds

Perhaps the most famous of Spain's wines comes from its most famous region: Rioja. Rioja produces some bold and delicious red wines, which primarily come from a blend of tempranillo, graciano, mazuelo, and garnacha grapes.

Tempranillo also goes into wines made in the Toro region, and Tempranillo wines from Toro get really jammy. They're called *Tinto del Toro*, or red of Toro wines and are worthy of sipping.

A different red grape—and subsequent wine—to try is the garnacha. The garnacha (also known as *grenache* in France) grape is grown all over Spain and blended into wines, but for a truly great garnacha wine, head to the Priorat region. Priorat Garnacha wines are big reds with big alcohol content and are pretty intense.

Whites

Spain has some pretty good whites, too. One Spanish white wine that is a must-try is the Albariño. Aromatic and flavorful, this crisp, white wine is grown in the northwest corner of Spain, in Galicia. Its popularity is growing by leaps and bounds in the United States, and it's also starting to be cultivated by some American vintners.

Another Spanish white wine to try is Rueda. Made from the verdejo grape, Ruedas are light, pale, and sometimes lemony and herbal. Some people describe them as similar to sauvignon blancs, and in fact, some Ruedas are blended with sauvignon blancs.

Appetizing Extras

In Portugal, the same Albariño grape is called Alvarinho and is used in Portuguese wines called *vinho verde* or green wine. Though made of the same grape, it tastes just a little bit different, a little crisper and sharper than Spain's versions.

Rioja produces some white wines, as well, called Rioja Blanco (white rioja), which are primarily made from the viura or macabeo grape.

One white wine that has recently been reinvented by savvy Spanish vintners is the Airen. Widely planted—in fact, the most planted grape in total area in Spain—this grape has basically been produced for brandy and unremarkable, dry table whites. It has never been known for its aroma or taste. Until now.

Though planted for centuries, Airen finally has winemakers who know how to coax out its flavors. A new generation of Spanish vintners have learned that to get the most out of this golden grape, it needs to be fermented at low temperatures, then blended, with a 90-10 ratio with another white grape. When this task is accomplished, the results are sublime.

Sherry

For something a little different, a Spanish sherry can be a great compliment to a tapas meal. There are three main types of sherry: dry, medium, and sweet.

In the dry category, we have fino and manzanilla sherries. Finos and manzanillas have about a 15.5 percent alcohol content and are pale in color and quite dry.

Medium or medium-dry sherries are either amontillados, which have an amber color and nutty, dry taste, or the darker colored oloroso, which has a 17 percent alcohol content.

Oloroso sherries that are sweetened are called cream sherries. But one outrageously sweet sherry is called PX or Pedro Ximénez, made from a grape of the same name, and is sometimes aged for decades.

Appetizing Extras

María del Carmen Borrego Pla, a professor at Seville University, describes sherry's history. "Few wines can lay claim to a cultural history as lengthy as that of sherry—which dates back to the dawn of time—yet at the same time trace their origin without resorting to legend or conjecture."

Cava

Finally, one must try Spanish *cava* or sparkling wine. While *cava* is made the same way champagne is made in France, *cava* is made from three different grapes: macabeo, xarel-lo, and viura. The different grapes give *cava* its unique flavor. It runs the gamut from sweet to dry, and the bottle tells the style.

Sangria

Sangria is perhaps the most ubiquitous of all Spanish drinks, but Spaniards never drink sangria at a bar. Sangria is, in fact, one of the ultimate party drinks—a punch made of wine, fruit, and liquors.

Authentic sangria is made in homes and sometimes with cheap wine, cheap fruit, and a little sugar or cinnamon thrown in for extra flavoring. For some it is the party equivalent of "wopatooey," "jungle juice," or some other potent concoction of various alcohols and juices.

But for others, making sangria is an art, and some families guard their sangria secrets carefully. In fact, if you use good wine to make sangria, your sangria will taste even better.

If you go to Spain, ordering sangria at a bar is an immediate sign that you are a tourist, but that's okay. When I lived in Spain—as an American student studying abroad—I went to bars and drank sangria with my friends. What I have since learned, however, is that most bars didn't serve me authentic sangria; they served me *tinto de verano* or red summer wine, which was a mixture of wine and lemonade.

Spanish Beer and Cider

While Spain is no doubt a wine country, *cerveza*, or beer, plays no second fiddle. Plenty of good beer exists, and many regional beers abound. A good Spanish beer also works well with tapas.

Some popular Spanish beers include San Miguel, Mahou, and Estrella Galicia. Beer sometimes is lightened with tonic water or lemon soda. When mixed with tonic water, it is called *a clara*; when it is mixed with lemon soda, it is called *clara con limon*.

Another wonderful Spanish beverage to try is *sidra* or hard apple cider. This is made in the Asturias region of northern Spain, as well as parts of Basque country and Cantabria. *Sidra naturel* or natural cider is a refreshing and tart drink. Not too sweet, it makes a great accompaniment to tapas.

Pairing Wine with Tapas

Nothing is quite so sublime as when food is perfectly paired with wine. Take a sip of wine, take a bite of food, and … ahh. With each bite, the wine seems to taste better, and with each sip, the food seems to taste better.

But achieving a perfect pairing can be a bit tricky at times. To find a good pairing, some sommeliers and chefs try several wines with a particular dish to see what matches up best. However, unless you have unlimited time and resources, that's not always the best course of action. But there are some principles, fortunately, that can help you sort things out.

The first guideline to keep in mind is that like attracts like. When working with foods and wines, this means similar flavors in food will bring out similar characteristics in the wine and vice versa. If you have a smoky, paprika-laced dish, you don't want to match it up with a light, delicate wine; you want a wine that has some oomph, some depth of flavor to balance out the smokiness. If you have a simple, seafood dish made with lemon and butter, you don't want an overwhelming wine that's bursting with flavor; you want a simple, clean, citrusy, and tart wine that will match its delicacy.

The second rule is that opposites attract. If you have a dish that's hot and spicy, pair it with a sweeter wine; the sweetness of the wine quells the fire of the dish. If you have something really salty, then you want something sweet or effervescent to lift up the palette.

To apply these two basic principles when pairing tapas with wines, first think of the flavors of the main dish you'd like to match. The thing about tapas is that you typically serve from three to six dishes at a time, and the flavors will be a bit different in each dish.

Pick out one or two flavors to accentuate, for example, the smoky paprika flavor of chorizo-filled *empanadas*. The dish itself is sweet, but smoky. A big Rioja wine might complement it—standing up to the strong flavors of the sausage. However, another way to go would be to pair it with a sparkling *cava*. The *cava* lifts up the palette, and *cavas* or champagnes are quite versatile and go with almost any food.

Another way to describe this is to try to match up the "weight" of the wine with the "weight" of the food. If the wine is too heavy, it will overpower the food; if the food is too heavy, it will overpower the wine.

When I pair up tapas, if I am pairing meats, I tend to go with a Rioja or another Spanish red. If I am serving seafood or poultry, I love Albariño. And for just about any dish, you can never go wrong with serving a sparkling wine.

Sherry wine also pairs up naturally with tapas. The depth of flavor of a really good sherry can enhance the rich taste of tapas. In fact, Natalie MacClean, a wine expert and author, recommends that overall, tapas can be paired with sherries or *cava*.

Sangria, of course, pairs up well with tapas. Because it is sweet, its sweetness contrasts with the richness of tapas.

Appetizing Extras

Natalie MacClean's website, listed in Appendix B, has one of the best online food and wine matchmakers I've seen. It's a good place to start if you're trying to pair up food and wine.

When pairing desserts with wines, one good rule to follow is to make your wine sweeter than your dessert; otherwise, the wine makes the dessert taste less sweet. A good alternative, of course, is to pair desserts with sparkling wine.

If you're using wine in a recipe, a good suggestion is to cook with the same wine you plan to serve with dinner, says John Schaal, owner of Vino 100. "That's not to say you should cook with a $200 bottle of wine, but if you're serving a $20 bottle of wine, you should also cook with it. You can go from okay to really good with just the difference of a few dollars."

And you don't have to stick to Spanish wines. Just as many of the tapas recipes in this book have an international flair, try wines from across the globe as well. Just experiment and see. If you are hosting a party, try out a few bottles of wine with a couple of dishes and see what works best. A few sips and a few bites, and you'll know if the match you're trying for works.

At the end of the day, though, if you're a red wine drinker and want to drink a cabernet sauvignon with your chicken, go ahead and do it. What matters most, in pairing wine with food, is that you like the wine and you like the food.

Sangria

There are countless variations of sangria, and every sangria maker puts his or her own personal touch on the drink. You can use leftover fruit, favorite liquors, and even different varieties of wine. But no matter how you make it, nothing is more refreshing on a summer evening than sharing tapas and a pitcher of sangria with friends.

1 red apple, like Fuji or Delicious, diced

1 orange, sliced, with skin attached

1 lemon, sliced, with skin attached

Juice of 1 orange

Juice of 1 lemon

1 bottle red wine, preferably Spanish Rioja

¼ cup orange liquor, like Gran Gala or Grand Marnier

2 cups club soda

Yield: 8 servings
Prep and Infusion Time: 15 minutes
Refrigerate Time: 1 to 2 hours
Serving Size: About 1 cup plus ice and fruit

1. In a bowl, mix apple, orange, and lemon pieces. Toss with orange and lemon juice.

2. Put juice and fruit mixture into a pitcher. Pour wine and orange liquor over fruit. Refrigerate 1 to 2 hours.

3. Just before serving, add club soda and stir. Pour sangria, with fruit, into glasses filled with ice.

 Tapas Tricks

I prefer using orange liquor, but some sangria aficionados prefer brandy while others add in a shot of rum or whiskey.

Variation: For **White Sangria,** substitute white wine for red wine, and instead of apples, use peaches. For **Sparkling Sangria,** instead of red wine, use Spanish sparkling wine or *cava.* Substitute club soda with passion fruit juice or another exotic juice. Substitute apples with berries, like strawberries or raspberries.

Nonalcoholic Sangria

Sometimes you might have guests who don't drink alcohol, and this nonalcoholic sangria is a great substitute.

4 tsp. granulated sugar

1 tsp. cinnamon

1 orange, sliced with rind

1 lemon, sliced with rind

1 apple, cored and cut into pieces

Juice of 1 orange

Juice of 1 lemon

4 cups sparkling grape or apple juice

1 cup cranberry juice

3 cups club soda or white soda

Yield: 8 servings
Prep Time: 15 minutes
Refrigerate Time: 30 minutes
Serving Size: 1 cup plus ice

1. Sprinkle sugar and cinnamon over cut up orange, lemon, and apple pieces. Mix in juice from orange and lemon.

2. Pour sparkling grape or apple juice, cranberry juice, and club soda over fruit and sugar mixture. Chill for 30 minutes before serving.

 Tapas Tricks

If you plan on serving this to children, call it "Grape Juice Fruit Punch" instead.

Tinto de Verano

If you order sangria in a restaurant or a bar in Spain, likely you will get this sweet drink. It's not really sangria—it's just a mix of red wine and lemonade, served over ice with cut up bits of fruit.

2 slices apple, diced

2 slices orange

½ cup red wine

½ cup lemonade

Yield: 1 serving
Prep Time: 5 minutes
Serving Size: 1 cup over ice

1. Mix apple, orange, wine, and lemonade. Serve in a glass filled with ice.

Variation: For an extra kick—to make this drink a little bit more like real sangria—add a ½ shot of brandy or orange liquor.

Spanish Screwdriver

If you like sherry, you'll love this drink. It's just sherry and orange juice, served over ice, delicious and refreshing.

½ cup sherry wine, preferably a dry sherry

½ cup orange juice

Yield: 1 serving
Prep Time: 5 minutes
Serving Size: 1 cup over ice

1. Mix sherry and juice. Serve in a glass filled with ice; garnish with a twist of orange.

Appetizing Extras

The regular screwdriver drink—a potent mix of vodka and orange juice—is said to have gotten its name from oil rig workers who would mix vodka into their cans of orange juice with screwdrivers.

The Least You Need to Know

◆ Spain, the second largest producer of wine, has a history of wine-making that goes back thousands of years.

◆ Spain has more than 50 different wine regions; the two to remember for reds are Rioja and Ribero del Duero, which get their richness from the tempranillo grape; Jerez is the main region for sherry.

◆ A great Spanish white to try is Albariño; Rioja Blanca is another nice white.

◆ Spanish sparkling wine or *cava* is wonderful to try.

◆ Sangria is simply wine, a little bit of liquor, and cut up fruits.

◆ When pairing wine with food, remember like works with like, and opposites attract.

Chapter **13**

Fiesta Time

In This Chapter

◆ Party planning

◆ Tapas dish combinations

◆ Presentation

◆ Adding music

Now that you've been making some tapas dishes, you want to share them with friends and family. Tapas, whether at a restaurant or at home, is not just a style of cooking—it is an experience to share.

Entertaining tapas style can be as simple as a summer picnic dinner for two or as elaborate as a party for hundreds. The principles for party planning are similar, whether small or big. This chapter explains some of the basics of tapas party planning, including tricks to make it simple and easy. It also includes some suggested menus and tapas dish combinations, as well as presentation and even music recommendations.

Planning Your Fiesta

All good parties start with good planning. Party plans don't have to be elaborate, but a little bit of forethought goes a long way. After you've decided your guest list and set the date, the next big task is to plan your menu.

Menu Planning

The combinations of dishes you can make for a tapas dinner party are pretty much endless, but a couple of guidelines might help you in planning your menu.

A good rule of thumb is to plan on making at least four or five tapas dishes: one cold, one hot, one dessert, and one salad. If you're doing five, serve one extra hot if you're entertaining in cooler months; in summer months, add one extra cold. In terms of quantity, plan on two to three appetizer servings per person per dish. If you are making a wider selection of dishes, then you don't have to make quite as much quantity per dish.

When you plan your menu, pick dishes you have previously made, or at least, don't make more than two new dishes for a party. I've learned that sometimes when I make a new dish, it doesn't quite turn out the way I want it to, and the time for kitchen mishaps isn't 20 minutes before guests are arriving. If you really want to try a new dish, practice it at least once during the week before your party.

Also, choose dishes you enjoy eating as well as cooking. And plan some dishes you can easily and quickly prepare to balance out those that require a bit more time or finesse.

And finally, think about balancing flavors. Some dishes complement each other better than others. Also make sure you have a variety of flavors. You don't, for example, want to serve three beef dishes or four potato dishes. Nor do you want three dishes heavily seasoned with paprika or four dishes enveloped by garlic.

I usually start with some simple dips and noshes—Marinated Olives or Carrots and a Chicken Liver Pâté with toasted baguette slices or Caramelized Onion Dip with Crudités. A bowl of salted Marcona almonds is a nice and easy addition to the mix.

Then I always plan a salad course. Because most tapas dishes, both cold and hot and even vegetarian ones, tend to be quite filling, a good salad dish can lighten and balance things out.

I usually have at least one vegetarian dish—cold or hot—and two different meat dishes. And I serve one dessert course. If it is a particularly large party, I might serve two desserts.

Menu Suggestions

If you get stuck deciding on a menu, try one of these 10 suggested tapas dinners. None have a suggested dessert as I believe any dessert—including non-Spanish ones—can complement a tapas dinner.

Menu One: Orange and Mixed Greens Salad, *Ensalada Rusa* with Marinated Tomatoes, *Bocadillas de Queso y Jamon*, and *Pan con Tomate*.

Menu Two: Olive Tapenade and Marinated Carrots, Smoky, Smashed Potatoes with breaded pork tenderloin or Pork *En Adobo*, Asparagus with Two Sauces.

Menu Three: *Tortilla Español*, Orange and Mixed Greens Salad, Marinated Olives and *Bandilleras*, *Empanadas* of your choice, and Chicken Breast with Rosemary and Cherries.

Menu Four: Karen's Crab Dip with a Spanish Flair or Caramelized Onion Dip with Crudités and crackers, ham and Manchego served on open face sandwiches, salad of mixed greens, salmon with sherry, and beef brochettes.

Menu Five: Stewed Spinach and Chickpeas, Creamy Olive Tapenade, *Gambas a la Plancha* (Grilled Shrimp), *Empanadas* of your choice, *albondigas* and a salad of mixed greens.

Menu Six: Garlic Soup, salad of mixed greens with Simple Sherry Vinaigrette, *Tortilla Español* or another tortilla dish, Pork Tenderloin with Sherry, Asparagus with Two Sauces.

Menu Seven: Gazpacho, Marinated Olives and *Bandilleras*, *Empanadas*, *Tortilla Español*, and a mixed greens salad.

Menu Eight: Paella Rice Balls with Saffron Mayonnaise, Lamb Meatballs with Romanesco Sauce, Gazpacho, Orange and Mixed

Appetizing Extras

One way to make a tapas dinner easier is to invite your guests to bring their favorite appetizer dish. Some gourmet groups also have one person plan the menu and then send the recipes to their guests to make.

Greens Salad, artichokes and avocados, Marinated Olives, and ham and Manchego plated and served with crusty baguettes.

Menu Nine: *Patatas Bravas*, Beef and Vegetable Kebobs, salad of mixed greens, and *Empanadas*.

Menu Ten: *Gambas al Ajillo*, Gazpacho, *Tortilla Español*, Olive Tapenade and Serrano Ham Wrapped Melon Pieces.

Party Prepping

After I decide on my menu, I divide the dishes—not in the order I plan to serve them but what I can make ahead of time. Any dish I can make beforehand makes things go much more smoothly. Though some dishes must be made the day of the party or just before my guests arrive, plenty of dishes can either be made completely or partially ahead of time.

Some dishes can even be made two or more days early. One dish you can make weeks ahead of time is Marinated Olives; in fact, they taste better the longer they are marinated. You can also make Marinated Carrots three days beforehand, and like the olives, they taste better if they are marinated longer than just one day.

Other dishes you can make a day or two ahead of time include: Carrot Dip, Caramelized Onion Dip, Crab Dip, Pâté, *Ensalada Rusa*, Meatballs, *Arroz con Pollo*, Gazpacho, Chickpea Dip, Olive Tapenade, Sherry Soaked Raisins, Potatoes with Alioli Sauce, *Tortilla Español*, and *Huevos Rellenos*. Also make sauces like homemade mayonnaise a day ahead of time.

You can assemble some dishes ahead of time, such as: *empanadas*, tartlets, Indian Beggar Bags, and egg rolls. If you make them more than three days ahead of time, freeze them or refrigerate them if you are making them only one or two days early.

Even salads can be made a day or two beforehand. Chop your vegetables, meats, and cheeses, but keep everything separated. Also, if you are adding nuts or croutons, add them just before you are ready to serve them; they'll get soggy otherwise. Make dressings a day or two ahead of time and refrigerate them. Do not mix the dressing with the salad until you are ready to serve it or you will have a soggy salad.

Make some dishes, including any fried tapas, the day of the party. Fried dishes taste best when they are made just before serving. Most meat dishes—*Arroz con Pollo* being an exception—should be made the day of the party, as well.

But even for dishes you have to make the day of the party, you can do some things to make that cooking go smoother. What really helps is to do all or most of your prep work the day before your party.

Simply dice, cut, grate, or chop your ingredients, measure them, and put them into separate containers in the refrigerator, and they are ready to go straight into your recipe. The actual cooking on the day of your party will be much easier, and when your guests arrive, you'll be able to enjoy them and your party because you won't feel so ragged from having cooked all day.

It also helps to have all your equipment and ingredients organized and ready to go before you start cooking. If you have your measuring bowls, spoons, ingredients, and knives where you need them, you'll spend less time tracking down equipment and ingredients. This kind of planning, what the French call *mis-en-place*, I first learned while taking a cooking class at Jill Prescott's Cooking School. It sounds really simple, but it makes a huge difference.

> **Hablo Tapas**
>
> *Mis-en-place* is a French cooking term that means "everything in its place." I like to translate it as get your mess in place.

Plating Pretty

Though you chew with your mouth, you actually begin eating with your eyes. Presentation counts, and your guests will enjoy your meal even more if you spend a little extra time making your dishes look as delicious as they taste.

When you serve olives, carrots, or almonds, place them in fun, little, different-size bowls. Keep your serving dishes clean by keeping a piece of wet paper towel handy, and take the time to wipe off errant drips from plates or bowls to give a professional appearance.

Sprinkle chopped parsley and cilantro on top of a dip, marinated olives or carrots, or pâté for garnish and extra color. When plating ham or cheese, add a bit of green to your plate. Mixed greens add some color and interest and make a plate look less bare.

Another technique I use is to sprinkle some dried nuts and fruits or fresh fruits between the cheeses or ham slices on a plate. They not only add color and texture but also taste, too.

 **Tapas Tricks**

Though you may not enjoy eating them, collard greens are both beautiful and sturdy. A caterer friend of mine loves adding them to her cheese and meat plates because they hold up well over the course of an evening.

When I individually plate salads, sometimes I place the greens down first, then put individual, neat, little piles of diced, shredded, or chopped vegetables into sections over the salad. I also love plating julienned vegetables, especially red and yellow peppers, in spirals out from the center of the plate. Then I top the salad with cheese and nuts.

There is even an art to plating canapés and finger foods. Don't crowd too many sandwiches or toasted bread points onto a plate. Stack them neatly into rows, and make sure your guests can grab them without sticking their fingers into other canapés.

Sometimes, I divide a serving platter into three or four sections, lining up different canapés for each section. You also can line up rows of one appetizer and alternate with rows of another. Again, use greens and chopped herbs or sprigs of fresh herbs as a garnish.

Be inventive and creative with your serving. Fill endive leaves with a tablespoon of salad or dip, and line them up on a tray for ease of serving. Put your shot glasses to work by serving tapas-size portions of soups or dips. Serve small portions of meats, cheeses, and other appetizers in Asian soup spoons.

Serve desserts individually in custard dishes on dessert plates or whole at the table. Whether individually portioned or served whole, sprinkle spices, like nutmeg and cinnamon, around the edge of a plate, and use whipped cream as a decorative garnish, especially if you pipe it out of a pastry bag.

Tapas Tricks

Use a squeeze bottle to create a decorative border. Fill it with either chocolate sauce or fruit sauce, and drizzle it diagonally across a plated dessert. Or use it to put small dollops—about the size of a quarter— around the edge of the plate. Then, draw a toothpick through the center of each dot, and you will get a ring of hearts.

If you are serving a buffet, you might print out small cards, identifying each dish. Or you can simply print out individual menus for each guest.

Finally, you've taken the time to present your dishes in just the right way, so make sure what your guests put their food on is equally impressive. Nice dishes and flatware on brightly colored tablecloths can add a festive touch. Even if you use disposable dishes and plastic silverware, use good, high-quality, and stylish accessories to complement your cooking efforts.

Setting the Mood With Music

The last piece to good party planning is music. Music can set the tone for your party, so you want something that is lively without being overpowering. A good choice is always flamenco guitar, which will add a distinctly Spanish sound to your party. Another Spanish touch would be to play *rock en espanol* or Spanish rock music. But if you are not fond of either genre, jazz and even mellow or light rock can get your party started.

Also keep in mind the tastes of your guests, musical and otherwise. Whenever my husband and I host a party, he will organize a specific play list that is especially tailored to our guests' tastes. Anytime you can show you are specifically thinking of your guests—whether by music or food choices (a special vegetarian offering for a vegan friend or a low-fat dish for a friend who's embarked on a new exercise program, for example)—makes your guests feel welcome.

And welcoming your guests and sharing a good time with them is what tapas is all about.

The Least You Need to Know

◆ Plan your menu ahead of time.

◆ Choose a balance of hot and cold, spicy and mild, and serve a salad and a dessert.

◆ Make whatever dishes you can ahead of time, and do as much preparation work as possible before the day of the party.

◆ Presentation counts.

◆ Have fun!

Glossary

bain marie A cooking procedure in which one dish with food is placed inside a larger pan filled with water. This also is called a water bath.

banderillas Little bits of food, skewered on toothpicks. Their name comes from the colorful swords used by *banderillos* (assistants to matadores) to weaken the bulls before the matadores come in to kill them.

blanching A cooking technique in which vegetables and fruits are plunged into boiling water, removed after a short cooking period, and immediately dunked into ice water to stop the cooking process.

bocadillas Spanish sandwiches—they come in both large and small versions. They are basically snacks to tide you over until your next meal, and they can be filled with anything, but most often are filled with Serrano ham.

borracho The Spanish word for drunk.

borrachos The plural adjective form of the Spanish word for drunk, but it also refers to a sherry-laced cake.

Cabrales Spain's most famous blue cheese.

capers The buds of a Mediterranean flower preserved in vinegar.

chickpeas   A legume commonly found around the Mediterranean. They also are known as garbanzo beans.

chorizo   Spanish sausage, different from Mexican sausage. Spanish chorizo is made into sausage links where as Mexican chorizo usually is not put into casings. Spanish sausage has different spices—often paprika—than American sausages.

cold pressing   A term used to describe the process of filtering or pressing olive oil. Before centrifugal machines were used, the olive oil was made in vertical presses. The first press—and best pressing—was known as cold pressing.

***Denominacion de Origin* (D.O.)**   This is a certification for food or beverages by the Spanish government that ensures that a product is the quality product that the label says it is. It is a similar classification like the A.O.C. in France and D.O.C. in Italy.

filet mignon   A French term that means small boneless meat. It is a steak cut from the tenderloin and sometimes is called tenderloin steak.

Iberian Peninsula   The most southern peninsula in Europe, it is the landmass that encompasses Spain and Portugal.

jamon   Spanish ham. The two most commonly imported varieties are *Jamon Serrano* or *Jamon Iberico*. Serrano is the less expensive of the two. Iberico ham comes from Extremadura from the Pata Negra or "Black footed" wild pigs. They live in the Dehesas among the Cork Oaks and primarily eat acorns.

lomo   The Spanish word for porkloin. It is the same piece of meat that Canadian bacon is made from. It is on the outside of the animal and it runs along the spine.

mahon   A cow's milk cheese made on the island of Minorca, it is the second most popular cheese in Spain.

Manchego   This most popularly imported Spanish cheese is made from sheep's milk.

Marcona almonds   Spanish almonds that are larger and more flavorful than regular almonds.

microplane   A new type of grater that makes it easier to grate cheese, chocolate, and spices and removes the colored peel or zest from citrus fruits quite easily.

mince   To finely chop something.

mis-en-place   A French cooking term that means everything in its place.

piquillo peppers   Small, extremely sweet red peppers, picked and roasted by hand in the Navarre region of Spain.

quince   Known as *membrillo* in Spanish, it is a common Spanish fruit, sort of a cross between an apple and a pear. It needs to be cooked before eating. It is also thought to be the fruit that Eve gave to Adam in the Garden of Eden.

quince paste   The boiled-down fruit, which comes in jellied blocks.

salmón   The Spanish word for salmon.

salud   The Spanish saying for "Cheers," which translates to health.

sweat   In cooking terms, it is sort of like sweating, in general. It is cooking vegetables over low heat, just long enough to release their moisture and flavor but not add any color to the vegetables.

tapar   The Spanish verb for to cover, and *tapa* is the noun for cover or lid. *Tapas*, therefore, is the plural form of the noun.

tapear   The Spanish verb that means to visit different tapas establishments, and the *tapeo* is essentially a tapas pub crawl.

tapenade   A dish made from mashed olives, olive oil, garlic, and capers. The word comes from the Provençal word *tapeno*, which means capers.

Tortilla Español   A classic Spanish potato and onion omelette; sometimes it is called *tortilla de patatas*, and it is similar to an Italian fritatta It is not like the Mexican tortilla, which is a flat, unleavened bread product made of ground corn or wheat.

Appendix B

Recommended Reading

General References

Andres, Jose. *Los Fogones de Jose Andres*. Barcelona Spain: Planeta, 2005.

Andres, Jose and Richard Wolffe. *Tapas: A Taste of Spain in America*. New York: Clarkson Potter, 2005.

Casas, Penelope. *Delicioso! The Regional Cooking of Spain*. New York: Afred A. Knopf, 1996.

——. *Tapas*. New York: Alfred A. Knopf, 2007.

——. *The Foods and Wines of Spain*. New York: Alfred A. Knopf, 1982.

Christian, Rebecca. *Cooking the Spanish Way*. Minnesota: Lerner Publications Company, 2002.

Cuthbert, Pippa. *100 Great Tapas*. London: Cassell Illustrated, 2007.

Mendel, Janet. *My Kitchen in Spain*. New York: Harper Collins, 2002.

Rosales de Molino, Cornelia. *Cuisines of the World Spain*. California: Thunder Bay Press, 2000.

Searl, Janet Mendel. *Cooking in Spain*. Malaga, Spain: Lookout Publications, 1991.

Websites

Delicias de Espana: www.deliciasdeespana.com. This is a great website to order Spanish delicacies.

Espavino (Spanish Wines): www.espavino.com. This is a great website to learn about Spanish wines.

La Española Meats: www.laespanolameats.com. This is a great website to order chorizo and ham from.

La Tienda: www.tienda.com. This is another great website to order Spanish foods.

Nat Decants: www.nataliemaclean.com/index.asp. This website not only offers great wine information, but it has a section in which you can click on to find food and wine matches.

Solera Restaurant: www.solera-restaurant.com. Technical Editor Tyge Nelson owns this wonderful Minneapolis restaurant.

Spain Trade Commission: www.us.spainbusiness.com. This is for hardcore Spain aficionados; it's mostly a techy site for business and trade, but their upcoming news section is great, and you can often find out about the latest Spanish foods to be imported.

Spanish Cheese: www.cheesefromspain.com. Everything you wanted to know about Spanish cheese.

Spanish Olive Oil: www.oliveoilfromspain.com. Everything you wanted to know about Spanish olive oil.

Spice House: www.thespicehouse.com. If you are looking for any kind of spice, this is the website where you'll find it.

Visit Spain: www.spain.info. This is the official site for tourism in Spain, and if you plan to travel to Spain, this is a great website to check out.

Wines from Spain: www.winesfromspainusa.com. This is not only a great source of information, but this organization also hosts Spanish wine and food related events around the country.

Index

W–X–Y–Z